Ezekiel's Temple

by

Mark Shipowick

TEACH Services, Inc.
P U B L I S H I N G
www.TEACHServices.com • (800) 367-1844

World rights reserved. This book or any portion thereof may not be copied or reproduced in any form or manner whatever, except as provided by law, without the written permission of the publisher, except by a reviewer who may quote brief passages in a review.

The author assumes full responsibility for the accuracy of all facts and quotations as cited in this book. The opinions expressed in this book are the author's personal views and interpretations, and do not necessarily reflect those of the publisher.

This book is provided with the understanding that the publisher is not engaged in giving spiritual, legal, medical, or other professional advice. If authoritative advice is needed, the reader should seek the counsel of a competent professional.

Copyright © 2024 Mark Shipowick
Copyright © 2024 TEACH Services, Inc.
ISBN-13: 978-1-4796-1706-7 (Paperback)
ISBN-13: 978-1-4796-1707-4 (ePub)
Library of Congress Control Number: 2023923259

All scripture quotations, unless otherwise indicated, are taken from King James Version, Public Domain.

Scripture quotations marked ESV are taken from The Holy Bible, English Standard Version. ESV® Text Edition: 2016. Copyright © 2001 by Crossway Bibles, a publishing ministry of Good News Publishers.

Scripture quotations marked NKJV are taken from the New King James Version®. Copyright © 1982 by Thomas Nelson. Used by permission. All rights reserved.

For more studies on Daniel and Revelation, the sealing
of the covenant, and the final atonement of Christ, see the author's
companion book, *The Final Atonement*, also published
by TEACH Services.

Table of Contents

Introduction		9
Chapter 1	The Return of Elijah	12
Chapter 2	The Great San Francisco Earthquake and the End Connection	16
	The Great City	19
	Spiritual Babylon Identified	20
Chapter 3	The Temple of the New Covenant	22
	Overview of Moses and Ezekiel's Temples	23
	The Ark and Ezekiel's Temple	23
	Where Is the Ark of the Covenant?	24
	Ezekiel's "Table That Is Before the Lord"	26
	The Priesthood of Zadok	27
Chapter 4	The Prince of the Covenant	30
	The First Fruits	31
	A Mystery	33
	Adventism's Historical Roots	33
	The Magna Carta Principle	34
Chapter 5	Unique Features of Ezekiel's Temple	37
	The Crystal Spring	37
	Jerusalem's New Name	38
	The Great Cleansing	38
	The Apocalypse Connection	39

Chapter 6	Daniel 9 and Mount Zion	41
Chapter 7	The Three Angels' Messages and Ezekiel's Temple	45
	The Two Witnesses	46
	Cleansing the Second Temple	47
	Worship Him Who Made Heaven and Earth	48
	Cleansing the Bronze Altar	49
Chapter 8	The Temple Mount versus Mount Zion	51
	The Prince of Zion	53
	The Roar of the Lion-Lamb	57
	The Gathering Time	58
Chapter 9	Revelation's Cleansing of the Sanctuary	59
	Cleansing the Golden Altar	65
	The Spring Atonement in Ezekiel's Temple	67
Chapter 10	The Apostles on Our Access to the Holiest	69
Chapter 11	The Daily Worship Services Compared	73
	Flour, Oil, and Wine	74
Chapter 12	The Daily of Daniel	76
Chapter 13	The Sabbath in Ezekiel's Temple	80
Chapter 14	The New Moons in Ezekiel's Temple	83
Chapter 15	The Gates	86
	The Eastern Gates	86
	The North and South Gates and Access to the Inner Court	87
	The Gate of Sacrifice	87
Chapter 16	What Days Are Holy?	90
	Holy Days and Gateways	91
	What Happened to the Missing Levitical Feasts?	92
Chapter 17	The Tribal Boundaries Redrawn	94

	Table of Contents	vii
Chapter 18	The Just Shall Live by Faith	96
Chapter 19	The Spring Atonement and Passover	101
	Atonement Week	101
	The Passover Theme	102
Chapter 20	Called to the Priesthood	107
Chapter 21	The Cleansing and the First Fruits	110
	The 144,000	111
Chapter 22	The Golden Altar and the Investigative Judgment	114
Chapter 23	The Judgment of the Living	119
Chapter 24	The Offerings of the People	123
	Burnt Offerings	123
	Grain Offerings	124
	Peace Offerings	124
	Sin Offerings	125
Chapter 25	The Corporate Offerings	129
	Balaam's Prophecy	130
	Hezekiah Cleanses the Temple	130
	The Goat Sin Offerings	132
	The First Fruits Replacement	133
Chapter 26	The Seven-Day Cleansings	134
	The Red Heifer and the Dead	134
	The Unsolved Murder Heifer	136
	The Cleansing of the Leper	137
	Ordination and Atonement Services	138
	The Nazarite Vow	139
	Purification of the Nazarite	140
Chapter 27	The Oath of Our Prince	142
	The Waco Tragedy	142

	The COVID Pandemic	143
	The Double Oath	145
Chapter 28	Preparing for the Latter Rain	148
	Conclusion	149
Appendix A	The Sanctuary Doctrine by J.N. Andrews	151
Appendix B	How to Study Ezekiel's Temple	155
Appendix C	Layout of Ezekiel's Temple	157
Appendix D	Table Comparing Burnt Offerings	158
Appendix E	Selected Texts on the Day of the Lord	162
Appendix F	Ellen White's First Vision	165
Appendix G	The Covenant and the Mosaic Code	170
	Freedom of Conscience in Ancient Israel	170
	Relevance of the Mosaic Code	174
	Overview of the Mosaic Code	176
	The Severest Punishment Is a Glorious Deliverance	187
Bibliography		190

Introduction

Ezekiel's temple vision, described in the last nine chapters of his book, has been a mystery to Jews and Christians for over two-and-a-half millennia. The layout and laws of this structure are similar in many ways to the ancient Hebrew tabernacle, but there are also many significant differences. And more intriguing still is the fact that after 2,500 years have elapsed, it has never been built.

The vision was given to Ezekiel during the captivity of the Jews in Babylon. At this time, the walls of Jerusalem were broken, and the city lay in ruins. The magnificent temple built by Solomon, the wonder of antiquity, was rubble and ash, and the nation's future was dark.

However, God had not forgotten Israel, and in their distress, He sent a message of hope to His people and, indeed, to us. This vision introduces into the temple service, for the first time, a new central figure: the Prince of the Covenant, the guardian of the temple and His people who restores the Promised Land to Israel, Jew and Gentile alike.

A message of hope for our generation, the vision illustrates the final, full restoration of God's people to their spiritual birthright at the close of human history by the Prince, the Son of David. In this divine allegory, God, in justice and righteousness, purifies the sons of Levi, restoring His kingdom and His image fully in His people.

In Daniel 2, the restored kingdom is depicted at the close of human history as a rock, cut out without hands, that breaks in pieces and pulverizes to dust all former and existing kingdoms, then fills the world, reestablishing the dominion of righteousness lost by Adam (see also 10:13, 21; 12:1).

Ezekiel's temple, with its structure and services, is a revelation of how that is accomplished under the outpouring and regeneration of the Spirit. As in ancient Israel and the early rains, the latter rains will fall at the close of the growing season, ripening the harvest—a type of the gospel's triumph and harvest.

The vision of Ezekiel has its parallel in the last book of Scripture. In Revelation 10, John, an emblem of God's end-time people, is told to "rise" and "prophesy again." To assist John, he's given a rod (or staff) and told to measure the temple, the altar, and the worshippers (see 10:11, 11:1). Like the powerful staff in the hand of Moses and the scourge of chords in the hand of Christ, this rod has power to measure and purge the temple of God. Ezekiel's temple vision describes in detail the measurement and cleansing of these same three objects: the temple, the altar, and the worshippers.

Although Christians and Jews have all too often not cooperated with God in fulfilling their commission, the Scriptures indicate that at the end, there will be a remnant, like John, who will cooperate fully, offering themselves wholeheartedly to His service. When God's people obey their commission to "rise" and "prophesy again," the Lion-Lamb of the tribe of Judah will empower and unify them in the truth, as David said: "The Lord gave the word: great was the company of those that published it" (Ps. 68:11).

This global movement of the word is depicted in Revelation 14 as a threefold message given in power "to every nation, kindred tongue and people" (Rev. 14:6). In the pages that follow, the relationship between Ezekiel's temple and these powerful messages will be explored.

First, though, a note of explanation: This book is written for the public. The author of the book is a Seventh-day Adventist. For non-Adventist readers, one unique feature of the book is its references to the dreams and visions of Ellen White, who lived in the late nineteenth and early twentieth centuries and is regarded by many Adventists as having had the gift of prophecy. I ask readers to approach these references with an open mind. The modern prophetic gift is never a substitute for Scripture, but if it is genuine, it is always complimentary—a lesser light pointing to the greater light of the Word.

One final note: This edition was also written with Jewish readers in mind. I ask my Jewish friends to reserve judgment until they've read enough of the book to see my reverence for the Torah. In the book, I argue from Scripture that Ezekiel's temple is 1) the temple of the Prince of the Covenant and 2) situated on Mount Zion, not on the Temple Mount. I ask them to look candidly at the evidence and consider the implications.

As the temple of Zion, Ezekiel's temple sheds a flood of light on the law and the ancient sanctuary ritual, illuminating their deep spiritual and practical meaning. Before dismissing that claim out of hand, I request, even implore, my Jewish audience to read Chapter 8 (on Mount Zion versus the Temple Mount) and Appendix G (on the Mosaic code) before reading the rest of the book.

Blessings and Shalom.

Mark Shipowick   1-1-2024

Chapter 1

The Return of Elijah

Behold, I will send you Elijah the prophet before the coming of the great and dreadful day of the LORD: And he shall turn the heart of the fathers to the children, and the heart of the children to their fathers, lest I come and smite the earth with a curse.

Malachi 4:5, 6

We are living in a transition time—a time of impending judgment. Like in Noah's day, lawlessness and immorality engulf us. In America and around the world, we are in a moral free fall. A primary reason for this is that the religious leaders and institutions of the West—Catholic, Protestant, Jewish, and Muslim alike—have not heeded the words God addresses to them. Like Pharaoh in ancient Egypt, severe storms, droughts, fires, plagues, and so on have little or no warning effect.

> "
> Like in Noah's day, lawlessness and immorality engulf us. In America and around the world, we are in a moral free fall. A primary reason for this is that the religious leaders and institutions of the West—Catholic, Protestant, Jewish, and Muslim alike—have not heeded the words God addresses to them.
> "

God, in His mercy, continues to call us to repent. But due to our insensitivity to the times, our spiritual deafness, He will greatly amplify these warnings in the future. Because God is love, He will do whatever is necessary to get our attention. The prophet Malachi forewarned us that in the last days, just prior to the "great and dreadful day of the Lord" (4:5), "Elijah" will reappear with a clarion call to repent.

In Scripture, we have a threefold warning and powerful gospel invitation to the world, which summarizes the Elijah message foretold by Malachi:

> And I saw another angel fly in the midst of heaven, having the everlasting gospel to preach unto them that dwell on the earth, and to every nation, and kindred, and tongue, and people, Saying with a loud voice, Fear God, and give glory to him; for the hour of his judgment is come: and worship him that made heaven, and earth, and the sea, and the fountains of waters. And there followed another angel, saying, Babylon is fallen, is fallen, that great city, because she made all nations drink of the wine of the wrath of her fornication. And the third angel followed them, saying with a loud voice, If any man worship the beast and his image, and receive *his* mark in his forehead, or in his hand, The same shall drink of the wine of the wrath of God, which is poured out without mixture into the cup of his indignation; and he shall be tormented with fire and brimstone in the presence of the holy angels, and in the presence of the Lamb: And the smoke of their torment ascendeth up for ever and ever: and they have no rest day nor night, who worship the beast and his image, and whosoever receiveth the mark of his name. Here is the patience of the saints: here *are* they that keep the commandments of God, and the faith of Jesus. (Revelation 14:6-12)

This invitational warning—the most urgent to be found in Scripture—is not entirely new. Laypeople and preachers in America and around the world delivered it with the convicting power of God during the second great awakening of the 1800s, and many genuine conversions took place.

This revival is also pictured in Revelation 10 under the figure of the angel who thunders a wake-up call to the earth. The prophecy states that this message was bittersweet. Although the people of the 1800s were stirred by the call to repentance, when Christ's kingdom was not established as soon as expected, the Christian churches again fell asleep.

This state of affairs continues until today, but according to the prophecy, God will give a final call. The church, embodied by the beloved John, is roused and recommissioned one final time: "And he said unto me, Thou must prophesy again before many peoples, and nations, and tongues, and kings" (10:11).

What message did John give? The measuring message of Revelation 11, a figure of the threefold warning and invitation of chapter 14. Like the early church, the preachers of the second great awakening gave these messages to the majority of the world in a single generation. Nevertheless, the reach of this future movement is still more extensive. Those who give the message are endowed with the latter rain, and their message is given in a power greater than that at Pentecost.

> And I will give power unto my two witnesses.... These are the two olive trees, and the two candlesticks standing before the God of the earth. And if any man will hurt them, fire proceedeth out of their mouth, and devoureth their enemies: and if any man will hurt them, he must in this manner be killed. These have power to shut heaven, that it rain not in the days of their prophecy: and have power over waters to turn them to blood, and to smite the earth with all plagues, as often as they will. (Revelation 11:3–6)

Some believe these two witnesses are Moses and Elijah in the flesh who are sent from heaven after the rapture, but this is an unsafe conclusion. Malachi urged the final generation to look for the return of Elijah *"before the coming of the great and dreadful day of the Lord"* (4:5, emphasis added).

Additionally, Christ's statement that John the Baptist was the Elijah of his day forewarns us that the final appearing of Elijah is not the literal appearance of the prophet. Instead, it is a revival message that comes in the final divine call to repent. It is critical, therefore, to understand the message because, as in John the Baptist's time, our eternal destiny hangs on whether we recognize it when it is given. If we understand the elements and content of the message, we will correctly identify the Elijah messenger. Our job is to take the Scriptures and look candidly at the content of the end-time call to repentance. Let's get started.

A summary of the message of John and the two witnesses is given below:

> And he said unto me, Thou must prophesy again before many peoples, and nations, and tongues, and kings. And there was given me a reed like unto a rod: and the angel stood, saying, Rise, and measure the temple of God, and the altar, and them that worship therein. But the court which is without the temple leave out, and measure it not; for it is given unto the Gentiles: and the holy city shall they tread under foot forty and two months. And I will give power unto my two witnesses, and they shall prophesy a thousand two hundred and threescore days, clothed in sackcloth. These are the two olive trees, and the two candlesticks standing before the God of the earth. And if any man will

hurt them, fire proceedeth out of their mouth, and devoureth their enemies: and if any man will hurt them, he must in this manner be killed. These have power to shut heaven, that it rain not in the days of their prophecy: and have power over waters to turn them to blood, and to smite the earth with all plagues, as often as they will. And when they shall have finished their testimony, the beast that ascendeth out of the bottomless pit shall make war against them, and shall overcome them, and kill them. And their dead bodies shall lie in the street of the great city, which spiritually is called Sodom and Egypt, where also our Lord was crucified. And they of the people and kindreds and tongues and nations shall see their dead bodies three days and an half, and shall not suffer their dead bodies to be put in graves. And they that dwell upon the earth shall rejoice over them, and make merry, and shall send gifts one to another; because these two prophets tormented them that dwelt on the earth. (Revelation 10:11–11:10)

We will look at this in more detail in the next chapter.

Chapter 2

The Great San Francisco Earthquake and the End Connection

In the spring of 1906, two weeks after the Great San Francisco earthquake, Ellen White was on her way back home to the Napa Valley from Mountain View, California, twenty-five miles to the south of the devastated city. Since the city was enroute to her home, she stopped there and surveyed the damage. She described what she saw as follows:

> Yesterday, on our way home from Mountain View, we stopped to take a view of the destruction in San Francisco. Notwithstanding some of the buildings were of the most stable kind and were supposed to be proof against disaster, the city is a ruin. In some places the buildings are sunken into the ground. This city presents a most powerful picture of the inefficiency of human devising and human skill to withstand the carrying out of the Lord's mandate. (White, *Manuscript Releases*, vol. 21, p. 91)

Providentially, on that day, White became one of the many witnesses to the great disaster. There is nothing unusual in her description; that is, there is nothing unusual so far. However, what sets her account apart from the testimony of others is that tucked within it, two paragraphs later, she made this somewhat cryptic but clearly prophetic statement of the future significance of that event:

Let all who would understand the meaning of these things read the eleventh chapter of Revelation. Read every verse, and learn the things that are yet to take place in the cities. Read also the scenes portrayed in the eighteenth chapter of the same book. (White, *Manuscript Releases*, vol. 21, p. 91)

"Let all who will understand the meaning of these things...." The meaning of what things? Of the terrible earthquake and ensuing conflagration that reduced San Francisco to rubble and ash. There is a divine connection between the deadliest and costliest natural calamity to strike the west coast of America[1] and Revelation 11. However, if we look at the passage, except for verse 13, which mentions an earthquake, on the surface, there is not a lot of similarity between this disaster and what is described there. Or is there? Let's see if we can begin to unravel the prophetic warning.

Before going further, it would be good to follow the counsel of the prophet and "read every verse" of Revelation 11 and also take a prayerful look at what it says in chapter 18.

Speaking specifically of Revelation 11 notice Ellen White said: "Read every verse and learn the things that are yet to take place in the cities." According to her, "every verse" of this chapter has an important bearing on future events. It describes things that are "yet to take place in the cities."

We'll come to that connection shortly, but first, let's look at the beginning of Revelation 11, which gives us the context: "And there was given me a reed like unto a rod: and the angel stood, saying, Rise, and measure the temple of God, and the altar, and them that worship therein" (verse 1).

"Rise and measure the temple of God." Intuitively, we know what that means: The house or temple of God, the church, is being measured or judged. "The time is come that judgment must begin at the house of God" (1 Peter 4:17). This is the same time to which Revelation 14:6 refers when "the hour of His judgment is come." The world, along with the powers that be and especially the church, all are arraigned before the bar of infinite justice. When? Judgment "is come," so the "when" would be now.

Think about it. Judgment day: It's here; and it starts with you and me, the house of God. Nevertheless, do we believe it? If we do, should our knees be knocking like Belshazzar's did on his judgment day (see Dan. 5)? Our knees shouldn't be if our house is in order.

---

[1] See https://1ref.us/mset4.

Notwithstanding, at the same time, we all should be somewhat weak-kneed given the magnitude of both the times and our sins. It would be healthy for us to have a true sense our great need of God's sustaining, transforming power. "Who is sufficient for these things?" (2 Cor. 2:16).

The implied answer to that question is "No one." None are able to stand in their own weak, fallen condition. Every man, woman, and child, from the weakest to the strongest, needs the sustaining, transforming power and grace of God.

Fortunately for us, this announcement of judgment day is inseparably linked to the everlasting gospel, which is not just good news but everlasting good news. A guaranteed victory awaits us, and not just a small one. The ultimate triumph is offered to us, the bride of Christ, as His Spirit is showered down on us.

Thus, God is measuring us, and that is the best possible news because when He measures a deformed character like yours or mine, there is convicting, creative power—a downpour of it—to transform us from deformity to beautiful symmetry. How? The Holy Spirit, the Comforter, comes to us, first as a witness against our sin but then as the restorer of our souls. His convicting power opens our eyes to our true condition, but at the same time, it contains within it healing balm. In the place of our deformity, He offers us the splendid wedding robe—the Lord our righteousness.

> Behold, the days come, saith the LORD, that I will raise unto David a righteous Branch, and a king shall reign and prosper, and shall execute judgment and justice in the earth. In his days Judah shall be saved, and Israel shall dwell safely: and this is his name whereby he shall be called, THE LORD OUR RIGHTEOUSNESS. (Jeremiah 23:5, 6)

Let's think about it for more than a moment; let's meditate on what the power of the Word made flesh can do when received; let's pray for it in persevering faith and act on our convictions, especially taking steps to set things right between ourselves and everyone our lives have touched.

This is so important because, as you can see from the text below and the unsettled state of society, there is stormy weather ahead, and we need to be prepared:

> And I will give power unto my two witnesses, and they shall prophesy a thousand two hundred and threescore days, clothed in sackcloth.... And if any man will hurt them, fire proceedeth out of their mouth, and

devoureth their enemies: and if any man will hurt them, he must in this manner be killed.... And when they shall have finished their testimony, the beast that ascendeth out of the bottomless pit shall make war against them, and shall overcome them, and kill them. And their dead bodies shall lie in the street of *the great city*, which spiritually is called Sodom and Egypt, where also our Lord was crucified. (Revelation 11:3–8, emphasis added)

The Great City

The "great city" of Revelation 11:8, where the two witnesses are slain, is spiritually called "Sodom and Egypt," but it is, in fact, Babylon the Great, which is styled the "great city" eight times in the Apocalypse (see 14:8; 16:19; 17:18; 18:10, 16, 18, 19, 21). We will review her identity in more depth later, but for now, we need to back up a little here.

Non-Adventists and those who are new to Adventism may not be aware that for many years, the church, like other reformed churches, has understood and taught that the two witnesses of Revelation 11 are the Old and New Testaments—the Bible. This is the meaning expounded by Ellen White in *The Great Controversy*. In chapter 15, she recounted how the slaying or silencing of these witnesses was accomplished between 1793 and 1797 during and following the Reign of Terror in revolutionary France.[2] During this barbaric time, the Bible was proscribed by France's revolutionary government, and atheism was made the religion of the state.

However, according to the text and White's prophetic statement above, these same witnesses will be slain again. A similar assault on the Bible—on the sanctity of marriage and the Sabbath—will be repeated as occurred in revolutionary France. Here is where the connection to San Francisco comes in.

On June 26, 2015, the Supreme Court of the United States issued its landmark decision on same-sex marriage.[3] On that day, five of the nine

---

[2] For more complete information on this, see chapter 15 of The Great Controversy. In it, White recounted how revolutionary France reduced marriage to essentially the same status it has in America today: a civil contract that can be undone at will. The same government implemented a new calendar, effective for twelve years, containing a ten-day "week" to remove all religious influences from it. In 1805, France reverted to the seven-day week. It is significant that France intentionally thought to alter the same two institutions given by God at creation: marriage and the seven-day week. For more information on the French calendar, see https://1ref.us/mset3.

[3] Obergefell v. Hodges, 576 U.S. 135 S. Ct. 2584 (2015)

justices of the court, like the revolutionaries of France, openly defied the Word of God and thought to overrule it by sanctioning same-sex marriage on the basis of it being, in their view, a fundamental, constitutionally protected right.

Of course, nothing could be further from the truth or the intentions of the men who framed the American Constitution. However, in the face of our own history, sacred history, and the warnings and objections from the four dissenting justices (Scalia, Thomas, Alito, and Chief Justice Roberts), the will of the five was imposed on the American people. In his dissenting opinion, Justice Scalia observed:

> This [decision of the five composing the majority] is a naked judicial claim to legislative—indeed, super-legislative—power; a claim fundamentally at odds with our system of government. Except as limited by a constitutional prohibition agreed to by the People, the States are free to adopt whatever laws they like, even those that offend the esteemed Justices' "reasoned judgment."[4]

Scalia's rhetoric is rather too tart, but his frustration and distress are understandable and well-founded.

Spiritual Babylon Identified

Regarding the harlot Babylon, that great city where the witnesses are slain, a woman in Scripture is often employed as a symbol of the church; In Revelation, there is an adulterous woman of an apostate church and a pure woman of the faithful people of God. To the extent that the unfaithful clergy and churches of the West—Europe, North America, New Zealand, and Australia—have turned from the Word of God and thought to change it regarding the Sabbath and marriage, the twin institutions established by God in Eden, they have become Babylon—the harlot—"that great city."

It's significant that the head of the largest of these institutions, Pope Frances, has given his endorsement of same-sex unions while at the same time denigrating Christian fundamentalists—those who take the Word of God as it reads. His hostility for Bible believers is, at its root, hostility for the two witnesses—the Word. They are in the crosshairs of both Babylon and the antichrist. The forces of apostasy forge, to all appearances,

---

[4] Obergefell v. Hodges, 576 U.S. Scalia J Dissenting, Page 5.

an invincible global world order depicted as the image of the beast, which all must worship or be killed (see Rev. 13:15).

Babylon, as she tightens her grip on the consciences of humanity, uses all the means of coercion she can muster, including false accusations of disloyalty and treason, the very things of which she herself is guilty before God. However, as in revolutionary France, according to this same prophecy, she does not relent in the face of sacred history.

> To the extent that the unfaithful clergy and churches of the West—Europe, North America, New Zealand, and Australia—have turned from the Word of God and thought to change it regarding the Sabbath and marriage, the twin institutions established by God in Eden, they have become Babylon—the harlot—"that great city."

Ancient Babylon, Sodom, and Egypt stand as lessons of the consequences of warring against God and flouting His Word.

With that said, what exactly is Revelation 11 telling us today? The two witnesses are sounding the warning: Be prepared. The scenes of the Great San Francisco earthquake of 1906 and the social convulsions of Revolutionary France, the twin Sodoms[5] of modern times, are about to be repeated in America's streets and in western civilization generally and for the same reason: Men have made void the Word of God. And would it be unreasonable to expect that when the divine measuring rod of Revelation 11 is produced again and "that great city" comes under the judgment of God, it will be announced in the same way: a seismic chain of events will shake Mystery Babylon and the world to the core?

---

[5] As in Revolutionary France, San Francisco has for many years been at the forefront of the movement to overthrow biblical morality and the divine definition of marriage. Regarding the causes of the social convulsions and anarchy that decimated France for several years during its revolutionary period, see chapter 15 of The Great Controversy.

Chapter 3

The Temple of the New Covenant

And he said unto me, Thou must prophesy again before many peoples, and nations, and tongues, and kings. And there was given me a reed like unto a rod: and the angel stood, saying, Rise, and measure the temple of God, and the altar, and them that worship therein.

Revelation 10:11–11:1

The second great awakening of the nineteenth century was based on the three angels' messages of Revelation 14:6–12, which combine the "everlasting gospel" with the "judgment hour" message. In 10:11, John is told to arise and prophesy again. After the awakening of the nineteenth century, John, a symbol of the remnant people, is recommissioned to deliver the original call, but with the added message of the divine measuring of the sanctuary—the church—and its worshipers.

The rod given to John is the enlightenment of truth that measures us in the same way Noah's message measured and judged the ancient world. However, we need to ask, If the hour of judgment has come—if God is measuring His people—what does that entail?

In a nutshell, God measures us by His law and shows us our great need of a Savior. The ancient sanctuary of the Jews illustrates this. The law, written by the finger of God in stone and spoken in majesty from Mount Sinai, was placed in the ark of the covenant, a gold chest that was covered by the mercy seat, a symbol of the throne of God where the Shekinah glory, His visible presence, rested within the Most Holy Place, the inner chamber of the sanctuary. This was the focal point of Israel's worship.

Overview of Moses and Ezekiel's Temples

We won't go into the details of the Levitical/Mosaic sanctuary here, but before going further, if the subject of the sanctuary is new (or even familiar) to the reader, there is a good summary of it in Appendix A by John N. Andrews that readers may want to review first before looking more closely at Ezekiel's temple. This approach is recommended because Scripture generally operates on the principle of "repeat and expand."

In the case of the temples, we start with the original Levitical tabernacle, and once we're familiar with its basic elements and services, we'll compare it with other related scriptures, such as the one below. Our goal is to better understand the ministry of Christ for us in the heavenly sanctuary, which God has illustrated in Old Testament types.

> Now of the things which we have spoken this is the sum: *We have such an high priest, who is set on the right hand of the throne of the Majesty in the heavens; A minister of the sanctuary, and of the true tabernacle, which the Lord pitched, and not man....* For if that first covenant had been faultless, then should no place have been sought for the second. For finding fault with them, he saith, Behold, the days come, saith the Lord, when I will make a new covenant with the house of Israel and with the house of Judah... For this is the covenant that I will make with the house of Israel after those days, saith the Lord; I will put my laws into their mind, and write them in their hearts: and I will be to them a God, and they shall be to me a people... For I will be merciful to their unrighteousness, and their sins and their iniquities will I remember no more. (Hebrews 8:1, 2, 7, 8, 10)

After reviewing Appendix A, I recommend Appendix B, "How to Study Ezekiel's Temple," which provides suggestions for a thorough, systematic study methodology.

The Ark and Ezekiel's Temple

While Ezekiel's temple vision has been something of a mystery since it was given five centuries before Christ, I believe God's people will understand it well before the return of Christ because it describes essential truths regarding the atonement and sealing of the covenant under the outpouring of the latter rain.

Recently, I wrote an article on Ezekiel's temple, comparing its services with the offerings and feasts of the Levitical sanctuary. There are many intriguing differences. The article included the table in Appendix C, which summarizes the differences between the various offerings. One reader emailed me the following thoughtful observations:

> I looked at the article with interest, because the temple described in Ezekiel has always been a subject of mystery to me for sure. Not only are (certain) feasts not mentioned there, but all the articles of furniture in the Levitical temple, including the Ark of the Covenant, are missing also. While there are priests, sons of Zadok, there seems to be no high priest (unless I missed it).

Down the line, we will look at these observations and answer these questions: 1) Where is the ark of the covenant in Ezekiel's temple? and 2) Where is the high priest?[6]

Where Is the Ark of the Covenant?

First, regarding the ark of the covenant, this person is quite right that the ark isn't described in the vision. Instead, when Ezekiel saw the glory of God come from the east and fill the temple, he referred us back to the first two visions he saw by the canal and of the city, which one can read in chapters 1–3 and 8–11, respectively, for a more detailed description of what he saw.

> Afterward he brought me to the gate, even the gate that looketh toward the east: And, behold, the glory of the God of Israel came from the way of the east: and his voice was like a noise of many waters: and the earth shined with his glory. And it was according to the appearance of the vision which I saw, even according to the vision that I saw when I came to destroy the city: [Ezek. 8–11] and the visions were like the vision that I saw by the river Chebar; [Ezek. 1:1–3:14] and I fell upon my face. (Ezekiel 43:1–4)

---

[6] Readers will get a better understanding of the vision by reading it through (Ezek. 40–48) and verifying, as they go, the accuracy of the commentary here. The author also encourages readers to study the points of the vision that are not covered in depth in this book, which are many.

As in his first visions, Ezekiel saw not merely the Shekinah glory that rested above the ark, a shadow of the glory of God; he saw the substance—the actual majesty of God, with the four living creatures that make up His throne—enter this temple by the eastern gates and fill the entire structure—the Holy and Most Holy places—with His presence. Nonetheless, the most appealing part of the vision is that having done that, God announces that this temple is His new *permanent* home with His people.

This temple should therefore not only fascinate us; it should appeal to our deepest spiritual aspirations because it's a promise of the restored kingdom—the return of the glory of God to His people—not merely in type, but in fact. Although the vision is an allegory, this event is literal.

The return of the glory of God to His people is the restoration of His image in them. This return begins with the return of the Comforter. The heavenly dew sent by God ripens the harvest and completes the kingdom and mystery of God: Christ in us, the hope of glory (see Col. 1:27).

Think about it for more than a moment. Emmanuel—God with *us* (see Isa. 7:14). What amazing love and condescension! This is not a distant promise; it is a current reality in every heart that allows Christ to enter it and be transformed. When we yield ourselves to Him, we become His temples and are "sealed with the promised Holy Spirit, who is the guarantee of our inheritance until we acquire possession of it, to the praise of his glory" (Eph. 1:13, 14, ESV).

Thus, the first phase of the kingdom of heaven is here for those open to receive it. For those who do, the Holy Spirit is the guarantee of the second phase "until we acquire possession of it." (verse 14, ESV).

> For this reason, because I have heard of your faith in the Lord Jesus and your love toward all the saints, I do not cease to give thanks for you, remembering you in my prayers, that the God of our Lord Jesus Christ, the Father of glory, may give you the Spirit of wisdom and of revelation in the knowledge of him, having the eyes of your hearts enlightened, that you may know what is the hope to which he has called you, what are the riches of his glorious inheritance in the saints, and what is the immeasurable greatness of his power toward us who believe, according to the working of his great might that he worked in Christ when he raised him from the dead and seated him at his right hand in the heavenly places, far above all rule and authority and power and dominion, and above every name that is named, not only in this age but also in the one to come. (Ephesians 1:15–21, ESV)

Ezekiel's "Table That Is Before the Lord"

Besides the replacement of the ark and the Shekinah glory with the actual throne and person of God, one of the most intriguing changes regarding the furniture of Ezekiel's temple is the replacement of the glorious golden altar of incense by a plain wooden "table that is before the Lord" (see 41:21–25).

This table functions like the table of showbread (or "shewbread" in the KJV) in the Levitical service, where the twelve loaves were placed in two rows of six each Friday evening at the beginning of the Sabbath, generously garnished and preserved with frankincense (see Lev. 24:5–8).

In the Levitical service, the twelve loaves of the showbread were also called "the bread of the presence" because they were not eaten during the week, but remained in God's presence until they were replaced by fresh loaves at the start of each Sabbath. In the same way the twelve loaves represented the twelve tribes on the north side of the tabernacle, the seven-branched candlestick on the south side symbolized the seven churches.

However, in Ezekiel's temple, the "table before the Lord" presents the end-time twelve tribes of spiritual Israel who are assembled on Mount Zion (see Rev. 14:1–5). We'll go into more detail on this in chapter 7. For now, notice Ezekiel's temple is not the only place in Scripture where we see a transition from one furniture arrangement to another in the sanctuary. We see a similar rearrangement in Revelation.

The focus of Revelation 1–3 is the seven candlesticks representing the seven churches (see 1:20). God has a message for each of these anciently and today, but when we get to chapter 4, like in Ezekiel's temple, there is a transition. The gently burning candlesticks are replaced by the seven blazing lamps of fire. Notice these seven lamps are not on the south side of the Holy Place where the candlesticks were but instead are before the throne in the direct presence of God (see verse 5). And, amazingly, they have become a physical part of the Lamb (see 5:6).

> Before the throne [not on the south side] were burning seven torches of fire, *which are the seven spirits of God*.... And between the throne and the four living creatures and among the elders I saw a Lamb standing, as though it had been slain, with seven horns and with seven eyes, which are the seven spirits of God sent out into all the earth. (Revelation 4:5, 5:6, ESV, emphasis added)

What causes the transition? Again, it is the gift of the Holy Spirit, the latter rain mediated by Christ. The dimly burning lamp of Laodicea (meaning "a people judged") is removed on the south side and replaced by the seven lamps of fire, which are centered before the throne. The result of this transition is nothing less than the illumination of the world with the glory of God (see Hab. 2:14; Rev. 18:1–3).

Just after this scene, in Revelation 7, between the sixth and seventh seals, we see the results: The tribes of the 144,000 and the unnumbered multitude are presented before God on the sea of glass, symbolized in Ezekiel's temple by the "table that is before the Lord" (see Ezek. 41:21–25).

The Priesthood of Zadok

Moving on to the priesthood and whether there is a high priest in Ezekiel's temple, this sanctuary, like the Levitical, is also governed by a law stipulating who is allowed to approach the most holy furniture - the "table before the Lord" and the bronze altar. By divine statute, only the sons of Zadok minister directly at the most holy altars (the "table that is before the Lord" is also an altar—see verse 22).

This is similar to the Levitical restriction that limited access to the altars to the priesthood and the Most Holy Place to the high priest, but in the latter case, the limitation was to only one man, and he only had access one day per year (see Lev. 16).

In contrast, in Ezekiel's temple, the sons of Zadok have continuous access to the holy altars *and* the Most Holy Place. The strongest evidence and assurance that this temple represents Israel under the new covenant is that no longer is the Holiest veiled throughout the year. Instead, its doors are wide open, continually giving God's ministers unlimited access to the divine presence.[7]

It is both encouraging and remarkable that in the ministry of the sons of Zadok, we see a class ministering and standing, like Elijah, in the direct presence of God. Recall that as Elijah pronounced judgment on Israel and Ahab, he told the king, "As the Lord God of Israel liveth, *before whom I stand*, there shall not be dew nor rain these years but according to my word" (1 Kings 17:1, emphasis added).

This continuous access of fallen but redeemed humanity to the throne of God is quite amazing, but there's more to the picture: In Ezekiel's vision, the ministry of the sons of Zadok is complemented with the ministry of the Prince, who is Christ. When the worshippers assemble,

---

[7] This also confirms that the vision applies post-1844, but for more on this, see chapter 9 (also see Ezek. 41:22–26; Dan. 8:14; Rev. 11:19).

the sons of Zadok apply the sacrifices, but it is the Prince who supplies *all* the corporate offerings. The good news is that the Prince does this for every divine convocation without exception and during all corporate worship. Also notice that on all these occasions, the Prince accompanies the people into the holy places of the temple in His role as both our High Priest and King.

Describing his unique role, God instructed Ezekiel:

And it shall be the Prince's part to give burnt offerings, and meat offerings, and drink offerings, in the feasts, and in the new moons, and in the sabbaths, in all solemnities of the house of Israel: He shall prepare the sin offering, and the meat offering, and the burnt offering, and the peace offerings, to make reconciliation for the house of Israel.... When the people of the land come before the LORD at the appointed feasts, he who enters by the north gate to worship shall go out by the south gate, and he who enters by the south gate shall go out by the north gate: no one shall return by way of the gate by which he entered, but each shall go out straight ahead. *When they enter, the Prince shall enter with them, and when they go out, he shall go out.* (Ezekiel 45:17, 46:8–10, ESV, emphasis added)

To summarize and recap, in Ezekiel's temple, the God of the universe takes up permanent residence in the hearts of His people. He rewards the faithful sons of Zadok, a symbol of both Christ and His faithful remnant, with the privilege and weighty responsibility of standing, not before a shadow of His glory, but directly before His glorious majesty, ministering at His altars.

> "
> In Ezekiel's temple, the God of the universe takes up permanent residence in the hearts of His people. He rewards the faithful sons of Zadok, a symbol of both Christ and His faithful remnant, with the privilege and weighty responsibility of standing, not before a shadow of His glory, but directly before His glorious majesty, ministering at His altars.
> "

However, these sons of Zadok are not alone. Michael, the Prince, supplies all of spiritual Israel's corporate offerings, accompanies us into the presence of God, and completes His final work of atonement in us through the latter rain of His Spirit. The end result is the completion of the mystery of God: Christ in us, the hope of glory.

Now unto him that is able to keep you from falling, and to present *you* faultless before the presence of his glory with exceeding joy, To the only wise God our Saviour [and Prince], *be* glory and majesty, dominion and power, both now and ever. Amen. (Jude 24, 25)

Chapter 4

The Prince of the Covenant

And I looked, and, lo, a Lamb stood on mount Sion, and with him an hundred forty and four thousand, having his Father's name written in their foreheads.

Revelation 14:1

In the Hebrew sanctuary, sin was expiated by blood. The lifeblood of the sacrifice sanctified "for the purifying of the flesh" (Heb. 9:13). In the true sanctuary of heaven, the blood of Christ washes away our sins, quickens and revitalizes our consciences, and restores our oneness with God. As our Passover and Advocate, Christ presents and applies His own lifeblood to our beings—the only effective balm of the conscience; the only remedy of the soul.

As we have seen, Ezekiel's temple illustrates this more completely than does the Levitical model by introducing the Prince of the covenant (see Ezek. 44:2ff; Dan. 11:22). Our Prince is the key figure in the vision. He is the One who establishes the covenant.

In sacred history, through the course of those human events in which God reveals Himself and leads His people forward, liberating them, it is always by the virtue of and through the atonement of our Prince. He is our door (or portal) to the future, and His blood is on its posts. In our response of gratitude, we present ourselves to God, offering our entire beings—body, soul, and spirit—like the ancient whole burnt offering—a living sacrifice (see Lev. 1; Rom. 12:1).

It is only when we yield ourselves fully to our Prince that we can then bring our best service to the Lord—the first fruits of our labors; then we can also bring Him our sins, confessing and forsaking them; and then we will bring our thank offerings and tithes. With that said, mark it well: All of these personal devotions are only acceptable and possible when they are offered on the foundation offering supplied by the Prince. He says to us today:

> Behold, I stand at the door, and knock: if any man hear my voice, and open the door, I will come in to him, and will sup with him, and he with me. *To him that overcometh will I grant to sit with me in my throne, even as I also overcame, and am set down with my Father in his throne.* (Revelation 3:20, 21, emphasis added)

Speaking of this privilege, the Lord, through the apostle, assures us:

> But God, who is rich in mercy, for his great love wherewith he loved us, even when we were dead in sins, hath quickened us together with Christ, (by grace ye are saved;) And hath raised us up together, and made us sit together in heavenly places in Christ Jesus. (Ephesians 2:4–6)

This is money backed by the gold standard of heaven, the law, and underwritten by the promises of God.

The First Fruits

> These [the 144,000] were redeemed from among men, being the firstfruits unto God and to the Lamb. And in their mouth was found no guile: for they are without fault before the throne of God. (Revelation 14:4, 5)

In Scripture, the pinnacle of the princely offerings is the first fruits of the crop, which, according to Revelation, are the 144,000 composing the 12 tribes of Israel—12,000 per tribe. In Ezekiel's temple, the "table that is before the Lord" is located at the center of the open doors of the Most Holy Place before the direct presence of God. Its function is to present the twelve loaves—the bread of the presence—which symbolize these twelve spiritual tribes.

These first fruits are a double gift: The tribes offer themselves willingly (see Ps. 110:3), but it is by the virtue and will of the Prince, who is the first cause of their outflow of love:

> Jesus Christ, who is the faithful witness, and the first begotten of the dead, and *the prince of the kings of the earth. Unto him that loved us, and*

washed us from our sins in his own blood. (Revelation 1:5, ESV, emphasis added)

In early 1845, in her very first vision,[8] Ellen White, then a tender youth of 17, was shown several things about the end times and the new earth. One remarkable feature of this vision is the central role of the 144,000 in end-time events. Specifically, she was shown that at the return of Christ, there would be 144,000 sealed, living saints.

Later in her ministry, White would admonish the church not to speculate on the exact composition of this group but rather to focus on the vision itself. Whether the number is symbolic or literal, the point is that at the return of Christ, the church that bears the message of the three angels and is translated without tasting death is this group.[9] If that's the case, isn't it time that God's people took ownership of that truth by equipping themselves and others to be among that number?

One of the most unfortunate, widespread errors among Christians is the idea that membership in the 144,000 is restricted and reserved only for a select few. This has been the common thinking among Adventists for generations as well, but it is not the message of Scripture.

It is true that membership in the 144,000 is conditional on our citizenship in the Israel of God, but this is the condition of salvation for all. The redeemed are all children of Abraham by faith. God has divinely ordained us for salvation and has made infinite provision for us by the Prince so that even the weakest can lay firm hold on His promises.

However, what God ordains, He does not force. It is still a matter of personal choice. The thought that we have a royal invitation and are divinely urged to be among this group to meet our Friend and Prince at His return should captivate us and animate our zeal.

Unfortunately, human nature shrinks from confronting the giants that occupy the Promised Land, but notwithstanding narratives to the contrary, it is a goodly land we are going to possess, and with our Prince at our head, we are well able to go up and conquer it.

---

[8] See Appendix F for the full text of her vision.
[9] Recently, a conservative Adventist leader suggested there will be many more people besides the 144,000 who will be alive at Christ's return. While it is true that the 144,000 may be a symbolic number, we need to be careful not to suggest that those who are translated will meet a lower standard than that of the 144,000. I don't mean to debate but only to caution that however a person views them, he or she should maintain that same standard.

A Mystery

> Just as soon as the people of God are sealed in their foreheads ... and prepared for the shaking, it will come. Indeed, it has begun already; the judgments of God are now upon the land to give us warning, that we may know what is coming. (White, *Manuscript Releases*, vol. 1, p. 249)

The mystery of the 144,000 has intrigued Christians for two millennia. One reason for our heightened interest is this group is especially associated with end-time prophecy and the apocalypse. The only book of Scripture that directly refers to them is Revelation. Here, as key players, they are pictured twice in some detail: Once, just before the seven trumpets; and again, just before the three angels' messages (see 7:1–8; 14:1–5).

Their placement just before these contexts is part of their mystery and appeal. The quote above holds out to us the divine inducement: "Just as soon as the people of God are sealed in their foreheads," the great shaking begins—earth's final sifting before the close of human probation. The only group in Scripture sealed at the end in their foreheads is the 144,000.

This is another confirmation that the end-time church are these sealed ones, and this thought should animate our zeal.[10] The depiction of the 144,000 just before the three angels messages is to encourage those who bear that message with the assurance of their ultimate victory and final reward.

Adventism's Historical Roots

As stated earlier, Adventism was born in the 1840s by the preaching of the first and second angels' messages by William Miller and his associates. Miller's focus, in addition to this, was the 2,300-day prophecy: "Unto two thousand three hundred days, then shall the sanctuary be cleansed" (Dan. 8:14).

The final cleansing and sealing of God's remnant by the atonement of Christ is the primary legacy of the Millerite preachers. It is the only doctrine that is unique to Adventism.

---

[10] It should be remembered that the sealing of the 144,000 does not place them beyond sinning. Every intelligent being, whether mortal or immortal, retains the power of choice and is free to transgress. Until we mortals receive immortality from Christ, we are at a disadvantage because of our weak, corruptible bodies. However, when Christ clothes us with immortality, we will no longer be subject to the temptations of the flesh.

Modern Adventists look back sympathetically on our pioneers who were sadly mistaken in 1844 regarding what the cleansing of the sanctuary meant. Miller had captured public attention with his teaching that the earth was the object Christ would cleanse by fire at His coming. When Christ did not return in the fall of 1844 as they expected; their hopes were devastated for a time. Nevertheless, in hindsight, the early Adventists were closer to the truth than they realized at first. When Christ entered the heavenly Most Holy Place in 1844, He did begin a cleansing work for the earth.

In Ezekiel's temple—in the symbolism of the Prince and the sons of Zadok—this work is better illuminated than perhaps anywhere else in Scripture.

The Magna Carta Principle

For most of recorded history, monarchs and despots have been the predominate bosses of human government. Thanks to the enlightenment of the Reformation, the nations where it took deepest root were elevated and acquired the ability to govern themselves directly without the tutelage of a monarch.

The common foundation of all successful, free nations is a principle called "the rule of law," which requires three things: 1) just laws, 2) an impartial, wise judiciary to apply them, and 3) a citizenry that is equal to the task of self-government, where the citizens are not themselves gluttons, drunkards, or slaves of lust.

Throughout history, monarchs have maintained their often oppressive laws with rigor. The administration of their governments were called "courts" because the prerogatives of the sovereign issued from them. The monarch himself was the highest court of appeal.

However, in Great Britain, this absolutism was ameliorated by the nobility who had maintained their rights and privileges, relative to the crown, for centuries. This salutary precedent was codified by Magna Carta in 1215, which, even today, remains a remarkable witness that justice is the first principle of all legitimate government.

Justice is above the sovereign because its origin is divine. It appeals to the spirit within us with the plea, "Let right be done." It speaks through the Word—the *logos*—which enlightens every person at the core of one's being (see Prov. 8:1–16; John 1:1–5, 9).

British recognition of the supremacy of justice, often called "natural law," was not only pivotal to Magna Carta; it was the formative influence in the development of the British common law. "Natural law" was again at work three centuries later when, under Henry VIII, the nation broke the papal yoke, placing the rule of law (justice) on a still more solid national footing.

During and following this epoch, as the Word of God was given freer reign, it worked great reforms in the morals of the people and the laws of the kingdom. Great Britain was proportionally strengthened and prospered. This was also the case in the other nations where the Reformation took root.

However, the prosperity of the West, rather than returning to God a tribute of gratitude and devotion, has had the opposite effect. In the twentieth century and especially since World War II, our Western clergy, churches, and universities have poured contempt on the bounty of God and trampled on His Word. Good is now called evil, and evil, good. Violence and vice are glamorized, while sports, entertainment, fame, perversion, wealth, and luxury are idolized.

Notwithstanding, all this was foretold. According to the ancient prophecies, when infidelity in the church and nation is greatest, God appoints his Son as Prince of Zion, saying, "Rule now in the midst of your foes!" (Ps. 110:2). And He confirms His authority by royal decree:

> Yet have I set my king upon my holy hill of Zion. *I will declare the decree: the LORD hath said unto me, Thou art my Son; this day have I begotten thee. Ask of me, and I shall give thee the heathen for thine inheritance, and the uttermost parts of the earth for thy possession.* Thou shalt break them with a rod of iron; thou shalt dash them in pieces like a potter's vessel. (Psalm 2:6–8, emphasis added)

Clearly, this will not be a good day for those who have resisted and despised their Sovereign's will. However, for those who hunger and thirst after righteousness, the appointment of a Prince—a Man like themselves, yet sinless and infinite—this is an awesome event in every sense.

Unlike the despots of earth, this Prince is a fountain of perfect justice and righteousness. His royal authority and power justifies and transforms His subjects. According to our indebtedness, need, and capacity to receive, the Prince distributes His gifts and graces from the sovereign bounty, which is infinite. Thus, in Ezekiel's temple, the Prince provides all the corporate offerings of Israel.

> *Unlike the despots of earth, this Prince is a fountain of perfect justice and righteousness. His royal authority and power justifies and transforms His subjects.*

Since the fall of Adam, the sealing of His covenant in us has been the focus, purpose, and ultimate goal of the Prince. It is grounds for rejoicing that the 144,000, soon to be revealed, are the first visible fruits of that ministry.

These early trophies are in contrast to those who have the mark of the beast. Rather than sealed by God in their foreheads, they are marked in the same location, or in their hands, with his number, 666 (see Rev. 13:16–18). And just as the seal of God is essentially spiritual, not physical, the mark of the beast is also primarily spiritual. The new world order taking shape in front of us, though unrecognized by most, which will brandish and stamp that mark, indicates to us that the sealing work of Christ is nearing completion.

In Revelation 14:1–5, the 144,000 are pictured before the throne. How do they come before God? I suggest it's by faith in the atonement of the Prince—by accepting the testimony of the True Witness and buying the gold, eye salve, and white raiment He offers (see 3:14–21).

These items are not optional, and knowing this, the True Witness—the Prince—pleads with us for our cooperation. He stands at our heart's door, knocking patiently, waiting for us to open the door so He can come in to eat and fellowship with us.

Chapter 5

Unique Features of Ezekiel's Temple

Earlier, I noted that Ezekiel's temple depicts the return of the personal presence of God, the open doors of the Holiest, the role of the Prince, and the high priestly work of the royal priesthood, the sons of Zadok. All of these changes from the Levitical service are wonderful in themselves, but there's more. The temple vision of Ezekiel is remarkable for a number of other reasons.

The vision was given "on the tenth day of the month," the Day of Atonement, "in the beginning of the year"[11] in 571 BC, fourteen years after the first temple built by Solomon had been destroyed (Ezek. 40:1). It was several more decades after this that the temple was rebuilt. Yet, when the temple was reconstructed under the direction and encouragement of the prophets Haggai and Zechariah, the first temple pattern and laws were followed, not Ezekiel's. The prophets understood that the vision of Ezekiel was a prophetic depiction of the end times.

The Crystal Spring

Its prophetic nature was evident to them in the crystal spring that flows miraculously from inside the heart of the sanctuary itself, issuing from the throne of God; this spring is a symbol of the Holy Spirit. Like the mustard

---

[11] The Hebrew yearly cycle begins on the first day of the seventh month. This is established by the Sabbatical and Jubilee cycles, both of which start here. (see Lev. 23:24, 25; 25:1–10.) Modern Jews hold this view as well. The Jewish new year, *Rosh Hashanah*, falls on the Feast of Trumpets.

seed with small beginnings, this modest fountain increases from a stream to a mighty river in the span of about one mile (see Ezekiel 47:1–12 and compare with the fiery river that issues from the throne of God in Daniel 7:9–10 and Zechariah 13:1).

The water in this river, like the fiery river of Daniel, is no ordinary water; it is able to make salt water fresh—a symbol of the miraculous regenerative power of the Holy Spirit.

Jerusalem's New Name

Another indicator that Ezekiel's temple applies to the end times and the messianic kingdom of Daniel 2 and 9 is the new name given to Jerusalem, its home: "The Lord is There"—a further assurance from God that He will dwell with us here eternally.

This name has its counterpart in the name "The Lord Our Righteousness" in Jeremiah 23:6 and 33:16, both of which point us to the gathering of the faithful tribes of Israel, when Jerusalem becomes the capital of the redeemed—the city of God.

> Behold, the days come, saith the LORD, that I will raise unto David a righteous Branch, and a King shall reign and prosper, and shall execute judgment and justice in the earth. In his days Judah shall be saved, and Israel shall dwell safely: and this is his name whereby he shall be called, "THE LORD OUR RIGHTEOUSNESS." (Jeremiah 23:5, 6)

> It was round about eighteen thousand measures: and the name of the city from that day shall be, "The LORD Is There." (Ezekiel 48:35)

> And I saw the holy city, new Jerusalem, coming down out of heaven from God, prepared as a bride adorned for her husband. And I heard a loud voice from the throne saying, "Behold, the dwelling place of God is with man. He will dwell with them, and they will be his people, and God himself will be with them as their God. (Revelation 21:2, 3)

The Great Cleansing

The seventy-week prophecy of Daniel 9 and the 2,300-day prophecy of Daniel 8 foretell the final cleansing of the heavenly sanctuary and the establishment of the everlasting covenant between God and His people. Ezekiel's temple emphatically points us to the same event.

In the Levitical model, on the Day of Atonement, the two holy chambers of the temple and the golden altar were cleansed. However, in Ezekiel's temple, the cleansing not only expands to encompass the temple but also extends to the bronze altar, inner court, and indeed the entire holy mountain of God:

> And he said unto me, Son of man, the place of my throne, and the place of the soles of my feet, where I will dwell in the midst of the children of Israel *for ever* ... This is the law of the house; *Upon the top of the mountain the whole limit thereof round about shall be most holy.* Behold, *this* [is] the law of the house. (Ezekiel 43:7, 12, emphasis added)

Christ is willing and longing to complete His atonement in us. The unbounded power and treasure of heaven, the Spirit of God, is available to us through the Prince. If His work has not been completed, it is not because He is unable to do it, any more than it was the fault of God that Israel wandered in the wilderness for forty years. Like Israel, no generation of Christians or Jews, so far, has willingly, unitedly cooperated with Christ in His atoning work.

However, according to God's word, in the near future, that is going to change. The prophecy says the faithful tribes of the 144,000 will gladly follow the Lamb *wherever* He goes. And because they offer themselves willingly, they will appear with the Lamb on Mount Zion, clothed in royal white raiment and sealed in their foreheads (see Rev. 14:1–5).

The Apocalypse Connection

Divine providence has juxtaposed Ezekiel's temple vision with his apocalyptic prophecies of Gog and Magog in the immediately preceding chapters, 36–39—another indication this temple applies to the end-time kingdom and supplements the Apocalypse. The verses that immediately precede Ezekiel's vision contain a promise of the gathering of all the tribes of Israel and the outpouring of the latter rain.

> Therefore thus saith the Lord GOD; Now will I bring again the captivity of Jacob, and have mercy upon the whole house of Israel, and will be jealous for my holy name ... Neither will I hide my face any more from

them: for I have poured out my spirit upon the house of Israel, saith the Lord GOD. Eze 39:25, 29.

The sanctuary of Ezekiel is the gospel in type, and if it is a powerful revelation of the gospel, then it will be accompanied by the testimony of the Spirit and ultimately the latter rain. The mighty angel of Revelation 18 who lightens the earth with his glory points us directly to the measuring of Babylon and the end-time church, the blotting out of the latter's sin, and its full liberation under the refreshing of the Spirit (see Rev. 11; 14; 17; 18). Clearly, God's people will become more intelligent at the end of time in regard to the sanctuary and the final priestly work of their Prince.

> "The sanctuary of Ezekiel is the gospel in type, and if it is a powerful revelation of the gospel, then it will be accompanied by the testimony of the Spirit and ultimately the latter rain."

Chapter 6

Daniel 9 and Mount Zion

Ezekiel's temple is a figure of the establishment of the messianic kingdom of righteousness foretold by Gabriel. Since the time of Christ, the rabbis have been in denial that Daniel 9 points to His first advent, but regarding the primary, end-time application, they hold that this prophecy *does* point to the final establishment of the messianic kingdom of righteousness (and Jewish world dominance).

They are partly correct. Daniel 9:27 undeniably speaks of an eternal messianic kingdom of righteousness where all earthly coercion is at an end and justice and righteousness prevails. This kingdom, disclosed in chapter 2 and reaffirmed in 7–9, is solidly confirmed in 12.

Evangelical Christians understand that in its first fulfillment, the seventy "weeks" are sabbaticals totaling 490 years. The rabbis agree with Christians on this, but to my knowledge, while they also give the prophecy a future application, none teach that, in the final application, the seventy sevens are seventy Jubilees.[12]

> Seventy weeks [Hebrew *shebuah*—"sevens"] are determined upon thy people and upon thy holy city, *to finish the transgression, and to make an end of sins, and to make reconciliation for iniquity, and to bring in everlasting righteousness, and to seal up the vision and prophecy, and to anoint the most Holy*.... And he shall confirm the covenant with many for one week ... and for the overspreading of abominations he shall make it desolate, even until the consummation, and that determined shall be poured upon the desolate. And at that time shall Michael stand up, the great prince which standeth for the children of thy people: and there shall

---

[12] For more information on this, see my Substack blog "The Abomination of Daniel 9" at https://mshipowick.substack.com.

be a time of trouble, such as never was since there was a nation even to that same time: and at that time thy people shall be delivered, every one that shall be found written in the book. And many of them that sleep in the dust of the earth shall awake, some to everlasting life, and some to shame and everlasting contempt. And they that be wise shall shine as the brightness of the firmament; and they that turn many to righteousness as the stars for ever and ever. (Daniel 9:24, 27, 12:1–3, emphasis added)

The reestablishment of the kingdom forfeited by Adam has been the first goal of every devout believer, Jew and Gentile, from antiquity. Christ taught us to pray "Thy kingdom come, Thy will be done, on earth as it is in heaven" (Matt. 6:10), and this was the desire of all the patriarchs and prophets: "O praise the LORD, all ye nations: praise him, all ye people" (Ps. 117:1). "For as the earth bringeth forth her bud, and as the garden causeth the things that are sown in it to spring forth; so the Lord GOD will cause righteousness and praise to spring forth before all the nations" (Isa. 61:11).

With that said, let's reverently look one more time, but in more depth, at how Ezekiel describes the return of the glory of God and the seal of the Holy Spirit that establishes His covenant and kingdom:

Then he led me to the gate, the gate facing east. And behold, the glory of the God of Israel was coming from the east. And the sound of his coming was like the sound of many waters, and the earth shone with his glory. And the vision I saw was just like the vision that I had seen when he came to destroy the city, and just like the vision that I had seen by the Chebar canal [see Ezek. 1:1–3:14; 8–11]. And I fell on my face. As the glory of the LORD entered the temple by the gate facing east, the Spirit lifted me up and brought me into the inner court; and behold, the glory of the LORD filled the temple. While the man was standing beside me, I heard one speaking to me out of the temple, and he said to me, "Son of man, this is the place of my throne [represented by the mercy seat in the Levitical model] and the place of the soles of my feet [the mercy seat rested on the ark, the foundation of the throne containing the law], where I will dwell in the midst of the people of Israel *forever*. (Ezekiel 43:1–7, ESV, emphasis added)

After promising to make this temple and Mount Zion His permanent home, the Lord goes on to explain why He brought Ezekiel to study this structure and publish it to the people:

And the house of Israel [including the new covenant church, which is grafted into the stock of Israel] shall no more defile my holy name, neither they, nor their kings, by their whoring and by the dead bodies of their kings at their high places, by setting their threshold by my threshold and their doorposts beside my doorposts [ignoring the difference between holy and common—good and evil], with only a wall between me and them. They have defiled my holy name by their abominations that they have committed, so I have consumed them in my anger. Now let them put away their whoring and the dead bodies of their kings far from me [that is, put away their idols, human and material.], and I will dwell in their midst forever. As for you, son of man, describe to the house of Israel the temple, that they may be ashamed of their iniquities; *and they shall measure the plan.* And if they are ashamed of all that they have done, make known to them the design of the temple, its arrangement, its exits and its entrances, that is, its whole design; and make known to them as well all its statutes and its whole design and all its laws, and write it down in their sight, so that they may observe all its laws and all its statutes and carry them out. (Ezekiel 43:7–11, ESV, emphasis added)

In the passage above, the Lord forewarns the prophet that when he shares the temple vision with Israel, not everyone will take it to heart. Some will not welcome the message because it disturbs their carnal slumber. Rather than awakening from lethargy, their love of sin and self overbears their love for God.

However, some will give heed to this powerful vision, and to these, Ezekiel is to present the full picture. God commissions him, like he commissions John in Revelation 10:11 and 11:1, to carefully observe all the measurements of the temple and present the complete design to those with ears to hear, including all its laws, the layout, and services, which are summarized succinctly by God Himself in these words: "This is the law of the temple: the whole territory on the top of the mountain all around [Mount Zion] shall be most holy. *Behold, this is the law of the temple*" (Ezek. 43:12, ESV, emphasis added).

Notice the entire area of Mount Zion is designated here by God as most holy.[13] This should intrigue all Bible students, especially Adventists and

---

[13] The temple location on Zion is indicated by it being on a high elevation on the north side of Jerusalem (see Ezek. 40:2), which, according to Psalm 48:2, is the location of Mount Zion. See chapter 7 for more regarding Jerusalem's two holy mounts: Mount Zion and the Temple Mount.

Jews, because it sets the standard for the divine kingdom: Perfect holiness. This is biblical Zionism.

In the very first vision given to Ellen White, the site of the temple prepared for the 144,000 *is* Mount Zion (see *Early Writings*, p. 18). Revelation 14:1–5 agrees with this. There, the 144,000 are gathered together with the Lamb on that mount. And this agrees with Hebrews 12 and all the ancient prophets: Mount Zion is the location for the assembly of new covenant Israel.

Inspiration invites us today by the visions of Ezekiel and the exhortation of the prophets and apostles to come in faith to Mount Zion; to the church of the first born who are enrolled in heaven; and to Christ, the mediator of the new covenant. Listen to the invitation of the Spirit and the bride:

> For ye are not come unto the mount that might be touched [Mount Sinai], and that burned with fire, nor unto blackness, and darkness, and tempest ... But ye are come unto mount Sion [not Mount Moriah, the Temple Mount], and unto the city of the living God, the heavenly Jerusalem, and to an innumerable company of angels, to the general assembly and church of the firstborn, which are written in heaven, and to God the Judge of all, and to the spirits of just men made perfect, and to Jesus the mediator of the new covenant, and to the blood of sprinkling, that speaketh better things than [that of] Abel. See that ye refuse not him that speaketh. (Hebrews 12:18, 22–25)

Chapter 7

The Three Angels' Messages and Ezekiel's Temple

Based on what we know from the first vision of Ellen White, the work of the three angels will be carried forward to completion by the tribes of the sealed ones who are alive at the return of Christ. Their work is also illustrated by the figure of the two witnesses depicted in Revelation 11.

In my book *The Final Atonement*, I cover the current and future applications of the seven seals and trumpets and make the case that these, especially the sixth seal and all seven trumpets, are the "overwhelming surprise" White predicted will suddenly confront humanity shortly before Christ returns.[14] Below, I make the case that we are specifically recommissioned as His 144,000 witnesses to give these final warning messages.

---

[14] In 1902, Ellen White made two prophetic statements indicating that humanity, before the return of Christ, will face a "great terror" and an "overwhelming surprise."

> Transgression has almost reached its limit. Confusion fills the world, and a great terror is soon to come upon human beings. The end is very near. We who know the truth should be preparing for what is soon to break upon the world as an overwhelming surprise. (*Testimonies for the Church*, vol. 8, p. 28)

> The time is nearing when the great crisis in the history of the world will have come, when every movement in the government of God will be watched with intense interest and inexpressible apprehension. In quick succession the judgments of God will follow one another—fire and flood and earthquakes, with war and bloodshed. Something great and decisive will soon of necessity take place. (*Life Sketches of Ellen G. White*, p. 413)

Since 1844, Adventists have been proclaiming the three angels' messages, but at some point in the near future, God will step into human history in a marked, unmistakable way. We need to be prepared for that so when it happens, we are in lock step with Him. By cooperating with God in sounding the alarm of the gospel trumpets, we not only save others; we cooperate with Christ as He seals us and are saved ourselves in the process.

In Scripture, the placement of the sealing of the 144,000 between the sixth and seventh seals is significant. I suggest the next major prophetic event to unfold is the Lamb taking the scroll in His hand and breaking each seal in rapid succession, which I believe has begun.

In fact, I believe we're close to the breaking of the sixth seal, but notice the sequence carefully: This seal is followed by the sealing of the 144,000 and the seven trumpets. As a refresher, here is what happens at the sixth seal:

> And I beheld when he had opened the sixth seal, and, lo, there was a great earthquake; and the sun became black as sackcloth of hair, and the moon became as blood; And the stars of heaven fell unto the earth, even as a fig tree casteth her untimely figs, when she is shaken of a mighty wind. And the heaven departed as a scroll when it is rolled together; and every mountain and island were moved out of their places. And the kings of the earth, and the great men, and the rich men, and the chief captains, and the mighty men, and every bondman, and every free man, hid themselves in the dens and in the rocks of the mountains; And said to the mountains and rocks, Fall on us, and hide us from the face of him that sitteth on the throne, and from the wrath of the Lamb: For the great day of his wrath is come; and who shall be able to stand? (Revelation 6:12–17)

The Two Witnesses

Sacred history shows that the forbearance of God has limits, but in mercy, He gives more than fair warning before His limit is reached and puts a check on the course of the wicked.

> Shall a trumpet be blown in the city, and the people not be afraid? shall there be evil in a city, and the LORD hath not done it? *Surely the Lord GOD will do nothing, but he revealeth his secret unto his servants the prophets.* The lion hath roared, who will not fear? the Lord GOD hath spoken, who can but prophesy? (Amos 3:6–8, emphasis added)

The warnings of the two witnesses of Revelation 11 are an important part of the threefold message of 14:6–12. In the first part of that message we have this divine call to repentance: "Fear God, and give glory to him; for the hour of his judgment is come: and worship him that made heaven, and earth, and the sea, and the fountains of waters" (verse 7).

Verse 6 summarizes the first message as the "everlasting gospel," which is global in its reach. It arrests the attention of all humanity by the announcement that the hour of earth's judgment has come.

The two witnesses, who are identified in Zechariah 3 as the "two anointed ones"—that is, anointed by the Holy Spirit—deliver that message in the power of the latter rain. Their plagues, like those inflicted on Egypt, are the evidence that the nations of earth are arraigned before God, the court of heaven has convened, and their hour of judgment has come.

Cleansing the Second Temple

After this first angelic wake-up call, two more messages follow. These will especially be God's means of measuring and purifying the church. This will take place in two stages, akin to the two cleansings of the temple by Christ.

> When Jesus began His public ministry, He cleansed the temple from its sacrilegious profanation. Almost the last act of His ministry was to cleanse the temple again. So in the last work for the warning of the world, two distinct calls are made to the churches: The second angel's message, and the voice heard in heaven, "Come out of her, my people.... For her sins have reached unto heaven, and God hath remembered her iniquities." [Revelation 18:4, 5].

> As God called the children of Israel out of Egypt that they might keep His Sabbath, so [in the third angel's message] He calls His people out of Babylon that they may not worship the beast nor his image. The man of sin, who thought to change times and laws, has exalted himself above God by presenting this spurious sabbath to the world; the Christian world has accepted this child of the papacy, and cradled and nourished it, thus defying God by removing His memorial and setting up a rival sabbath. (White, Manuscript Releases, vol. 2, p. 228)

Worship Him Who Made Heaven and Earth

The messages of these strong angels condemn the sins and doctrines of Babylon: doctrines that purport to overrule and change the law of God. The first of these is a call to worship the Creator (see Rev. 14:6). This message is given when people are rewriting the building blocks of life, the DNA, and mandating that everyone yield their bodies to a genetically altered vaccine.[15] However, the angels protest this arrogation of authority and infringement of conscience, warning that plagues and calamities are the result of transgression, just as the flood was a judgment on the wicked.

According to the climatologists of Noah's day, the flood was scientifically impossible because, until then, it had never rained. However, when the rain started to fall for the first time, the scientists and scoffers became believers, but they were too late.

Pharaoh displayed the same mindset. He attributed the plagues to natural causes, including the death of his eldest son, until the sea closed over him as it closed over the antediluvians.

Like Noah, the three angels sound the final warning and call humanity to repentance. Their message is reenforced by the testimony of the two witnesses who plague Babylon with ever greater scourges.

This is illustrated in Zechariah's vision of the two-sided flying roll—the law of God:

> Then again I lifted up mine eyes, and saw, and, behold, a flying roll. And he said unto me, What seest thou? And I answered, I see a flying roll; the length thereof is twenty cubits, and the breadth thereof ten cubits. Then said he unto me, This is the curse that goeth forth over the face of the whole land: for every one that stealeth shall be cut off on the one side according to it; and every one that sweareth shall be cut off on the other side according to it. I will cause it to go forth, saith Jehovah of hosts, and it shall enter into the house of the thief, and into the house of him that sweareth falsely by my name; and it shall abide in the midst of his house, and shall consume it with the timber thereof and the stones thereof. (Zechariah 5:1–4)

---

[15] The World Health Organization claims that mRNA vaccines do not alter the DNA of humans, but there is growing evidence that this is not the case—that the vaccines do promote the mutation of genes in a significant portion of the recipients. Regardless, no one denies the active agents in the vaccines themselves are genetically altered. See chapter 27 for more on this.

The purpose of the plagues is to both warn the unfaithful and test the faith of genuine believers. All who obey the call to leave Babylon and sever their connection with her are brought into harmony with God. Those who reject it are measured, weighed in the balance, and cleansed from the sanctuary and spiritual Israel.

Consider this statement from Scripture, which also describes the work of both the three angels and the two witnesses:

> Behold, I will send my messenger, and he shall prepare the way before me: and *the Lord, whom ye seek, shall suddenly come to his temple, even the messenger of the covenant, whom ye delight in: behold, he shall come, saith the LORD of hosts. But who may abide the day of his coming? and who shall stand when he appeareth? for he is like a refiner's fire, and like fullers' soap: And he shall sit as a refiner and purifier of silver: and he shall purify the sons of Levi, and purge them as gold and silver, that they may offer unto the LORD an offering in righteousness.... And I will come near to you to judgment;* and I will be a swift witness against the sorcerers, and against the adulterers, and against false swearers, and against those that oppress the hireling in his wages, the widow, and the fatherless, and that turn aside the stranger from his right, and fear not me, saith the LORD of hosts. (Malachi 3:1–6, emphasis added)

This prophecy describes the end times, when the Lord inspects His temple, measures it, and cleanses it. He will purify its priesthood, the spiritual sons of Levi.

Cleansing the Bronze Altar

In Ezekiel's temple, this is portrayed in the cleansing and dedication of the bronze altar and the priesthood. It is not quoted here to encourage readers to study it for themselves (see 43:18–27). After reading it, notice 1) that the altar and priesthood are cleansed and dedicated before the regular services commence and 2) the sin offering for the seven-day ordination service is a goat rather than a bull,[16] indicating the priesthood cannot officiate until the full service is complete.

Today, this ordination is open to both men and women, provided they each accept their divinely assigned roles and responsibilities. Like the ordination of the sons of Zadok, the cleansing foretold by Malachi applies to the church who are in receipt of the latter rain, washed in the river flowing from the throne—channels of the divine glory. May God help us to be found among them, with our lamps trimmed and burning.

> And he said unto me, It is done. I am Alpha and Omega, the beginning and the end. I will give unto him that is athirst of the fountain of the water of life freely. He that overcometh shall inherit all things; and I will be his God, and he shall be my son. (Revelation 21:6, 7)

---

[16] Under Levitical law, while a goat is the sin offering of the common people, a bull is used exclusively for the priesthood. For more on this, see Leviticus 4–9 and 16.

Chapter 8

The Temple Mount versus Mount Zion

From ancient times through today, Jerusalem contains two holy mountains: Mount Moriah, known as the Temple Mount, site of the first and second temples; and Mount Zion, the prominent elevation of the sector of Jerusalem known anciently as the "City of David." One of the mysteries of Scripture is the divine preference for Mount Zion over the Temple Mount.

It seems almost contradictory that from the time Solomon dedicated the temple and the glory of God filled it, the ancient prophets, without exception, regarded Zion, not the Temple Mount, as the chosen site of God's throne, preeminent above all others. To understand how that can be, we need to know some historical background.

Jerusalem is a most ancient city. It thrived in the days of Abraham when it was called "Salem," ruled by the benevolent priest-king Melchizedek (see Gen. 14:18). At the time Abraham offered his son Isaac on Mount Moriah, the mount was not far from Salem, but it was not yet part of the city like it is today.

Eight hundred years after Abraham's test of faith, Solomon built the first temple on this site, which was still not part of the city. Just before the temple was built, the site had been a threshing floor King David purchased at the direction of God to offer sacrifices in order to stop a deadly plague, which he had brought on the people by numbering them, contrary to the provisions of the law.

Following God's directions given him by the prophet Gad, the repentant king built an altar on this threshing floor, humbling himself and interceding for himself and Israel. The Lord heard the earnest prayers of David. He answered him by fire that came down from heaven, consumed his offerings, and stayed the plague (see 1 Chron. 21:16–27).

Some years later, when David's son Solomon completed the temple here and it was being dedicated, he took the ark of the covenant from the tabernacle his father had pitched on Mount Zion and brought it to its new home:

> Then Solomon assembled the elders of Israel, and all the heads of the tribes, the chief of the fathers of the children of Israel, unto Jerusalem, to bring up the Ark of the Covenant of the LORD out of the city of David, which is Zion.... And the priests brought in the Ark of the Covenant of the LORD unto his place, to the oracle of the house, into the most holy place, even under the wings of the cherubims. (2 Chronicles 5:2, 7)

The movement of the ark of the covenant from Zion to the former threshing floor, now the temple, was an acted parable that explains the mystery of the two mountains and God's preference for Mount Zion. Mount Moriah was the temporary resting place of the ark, a threshing floor; Mount Zion is its original home and, under the new covenant, its permanent resting place. [17]

Speaking of the immutability of Zion, David said:

> Arise, O LORD, into thy rest; thou, and the ark of thy strength. Let thy priests be clothed with righteousness; and let thy saints shout for joy.... For the LORD hath chosen Zion; he hath desired it for his habitation. This is my rest for ever: here will I dwell; for I have desired it. (Psalm 132:8, 9, 13, 14)

Isaiah and the other prophets confirmed the same. Notice below how Isaiah's prophecies of the last days predict the restoration of Zion as the city of God and the exaltation of Zion above all the hills, including the Temple Mount. Like David, Isaiah told us Zion, not Moriah, is the resting

---

[17] When the Babylonian army was about to destroy Jerusalem, the prophet Jeremiah hid the ark in a cave and, according to Ellen White, it is still there where he deposited it, undisturbed. A likely current location of it, therefore, is under Mount Zion because the prophecies indicate that in the latter days, the law will go forth from Zion (see Isa. 2:3; Mic. 4:2). Modern archeologists are divided on the location of Zion, but according to Psalm 48:2 and Isaiah 2:3, it is the highest elevation on the north side of the city—probably the site of the crucifixion.

place of the throne of God, the site of worship of all people, Jew and Gentile, and in the last days, the law will issue from it:

> And it shall come to pass in the last days, that the mountain of the LORD'S house shall be established in the top of the mountains, and shall be exalted above the hills; *and all nations shall flow unto it.* And many people shall go and say, Come ye, and let us go up to the mountain of the LORD, to the house of the God of Jacob; and he will teach us of his ways, and we will walk in his paths: for out of Zion shall go forth the law, and the word of the LORD from Jerusalem. And he shall judge among the nations, and shall rebuke many people. (Isaiah 2:2–4)

This agrees with many other scriptures that also point to Ezekiel's temple, situated on Zion, as the oracle of God. It's location on Zion is not stated directly in the vision, but the conclusion is inescapable because this mountain is "very high" and on the north side of the city (see Ezek. 40:2–5).

In contrast, the Temple Mount is lower and on the east side of the city. Furthermore, this agrees with the prophetic restoration of the house of David (see Zech. 3:8; 6:1; Isa. 11:1). We'll soon look at other pertinent passages that point to Ezekiel's temple as the temple and palace of the Prince of the covenant.

The Prince of Zion

Christ's claim to be the Son of God was repeatedly challenged by the Jews, who left no stone unturned to unmask the supposed impostor. One technique they frequently employed was to ply Him with difficult questions. At one of these verbal exchanges, Christ turned the tables and put a difficult question to them:

> While the Pharisees were gathered together, Jesus asked them, Saying, What think ye of Christ? whose son is he? They say unto him, The Son of David. He saith unto them, How then doth David in spirit call him Lord, saying, The LORD said unto my Lord, Sit thou on my right hand, till I make thine enemies thy footstool? If David then call him Lord, how is he his son? And no man was able to answer him a word, neither durst any man from that day forth ask him any more questions. (Matthew 22:41–46)

Christ referred the Jews to Psalm 110:1. In verse 4, this Son of David is not only a prince but also a priest, not after the order of Levi but after the order of Melchizedek:

> Thy people shall be willing in the day of thy power, in the beauties of holiness from the womb of the morning: thou hast the dew of thy youth. The LORD hath sworn, and will not repent, Thou art a priest for ever after the order of Melchizedek. (Psalm 110:3, 4)

The unique characteristic of Melchizedek, apart from not being a descendant of Aaron (Melchizedek lived hundreds of years before him), is that, unlike the Levitical priesthood, he is both priest and king: priest of the Most High God and king of Salem—Jerusalem (see Gen. 14:18).

In fulfillment of this prophecy, just before His crucifixion, Christ, a descendant of the royal line, entered Jerusalem as its rightful priest-king and cleansed the temple a second time. By that act, Christ attested one last time to His authority as One who has a triple claim on our souls: our Creator, our Redeemer, and our King.

The kingship of Christ becomes more important at the end, when it is critical to follow the Prince as our Commander in Chief. His role is depicted throughout the vision of Ezekiel and in many other ancient prophecies as the Prince who rules from Zion. He is that prophet-priest-king of whom Moses spoke and whom spiritual Israel will obey in all things.

> The LORD your God will raise up for you a prophet like me from among you, from your brothers—it is to him you shall listen ... And I will put my words in his mouth, and he shall speak to them all that I command him. And whoever will not listen to my words that he shall speak in my name, I myself will require it of him. (Deuteronomy 18:15, 18, 19, ESV)

The close connection between the ministry of Christ in heaven and His kingship over final events on earth is a theme that runs throughout both Daniel and Revelation. In both, the scenes alternate between apocalyptic events on earth and corresponding scenes of judgment and intercession by the Prince of the covenant in heaven.

Today, the Spirit of God invites us, Jew and Gentile, to participate in the victory of our Prince. The prophecies forewarn that there is rough weather ahead. To make it through, we need an experienced general with the heart of a lion. He invites us today to share in His glorious conquests (see Dan. 11:22; Rev. 19:11–20).

Before leaving this topic, here are some more selected scriptures (there are many more) from the Psalms on the preeminence of Mount Zion[18] and its king:

- Psalm 2:6—"As for me, I have set my king on Zion, my holy hill."

- Psalm 9:11—"Sing praises to the LORD, who sits enthroned in Zion! Tell among the peoples his deeds!"

- Psalm 14:7—"Oh, that salvation for Israel would come out of Zion! When the LORD restores the fortunes of his people, let Jacob rejoice, let Israel be glad."

- Psalm 20:2—"May he send you help from the sanctuary and give you support from Zion!"

- Psalm 48:11—"Let Mount Zion be glad! Let the daughters of Judah rejoice because of your judgments!

- Psalm 50:2—"Out of Zion, the perfection of beauty, God shines forth."

- Psalm 74:2—"Remember your congregation, which you have purchased of old, which you have redeemed to be the tribe of your heritage! Remember Mount Zion, where you have dwelt."

- Psalm 76:2—"His abode has been established in Salem, his dwelling place in Zion."

- Psalm 78:68—"but he chose the tribe of Judah, Mount Zion, which he loves."

- Psalm 84:7—"They go from strength to strength; each one appears before God in Zion."

- Psalm 87:2—"the LORD loves the gates of Zion more than all the dwelling places of Jacob."

- Psalm 87:5—"And of Zion it shall be said, "This one and that one were born in her"; for the Most High himself will establish her."

---

[18] The Temple Mount is the most contested piece of real estate in the world, anciently and today. It's considered sacred by all three Abrahamic faiths: Islam, Judaism, and Christianity. However, if the leaders of these religions were willing to accept the testimony of Scripture, that this mount was only a temporary sanctuary for the ark, compared with Mount Zion, its permanent home, the tensions would cease.

- Psalm 97:8—"Zion hears and is glad, and the daughters of Judah rejoice, because of your judgments, O LORD."

- Psalm 99:2—"The LORD is great in Zion; he is exalted over all the peoples."

- Psalm 102:13—"You will arise and have pity on Zion; it is the time to favor her; the appointed time has come."

- Psalm 102:16—"For the LORD builds up Zion; he appears in his glory."

- Psalm 102:21—"that they may declare in Zion the name of the LORD, and in Jerusalem his praise."

- Psalm 110:2—"The LORD sends forth from Zion your mighty scepter. Rule in the midst of your enemies!"

- Psalm 125:1—"Those who trust in the LORD are like Mount Zion, which cannot be moved, but abides forever" (ESV)

To close this section, I quote the prophecies of Isaiah, who, except for David, referred more to Zion than did any other prophet. Here are just three of his end-time prophecies of Zion:

> How beautiful upon the mountains are the feet of him who brings good news, who publishes peace, who brings good news of happiness, who publishes salvation, who says to Zion, "Your God reigns." (Isaiah 52:7)

> For Zion's sake will I not hold my peace, and for Jerusalem's sake I will not rest, until the righteousness thereof go forth as brightness, and the salvation thereof as a lamp that burneth. (Isaiah 62:1)

> Who hath heard such a thing? who hath seen such things? Shall the earth be made to bring forth in one day? or shall a nation be born at once? for as soon as Zion travailed, she brought forth her children. (Isaiah 66:8)

Notice in the last prophecy above that we have a picture of the labor pains and persecution of Zion and the birth of her children, a whole nation, that is suddenly born all at once. Quite amazing and unprecedented! Since this occurs in the end times, what nation can this be except the twelve spiritual tribes of Israel that appear suddenly on Mount Zion with the Lamb? (see also Rev. 14:1–5).

The Roar of the Lion-Lamb

The foundation of the throne and government of God is His justice and righteousness manifested in the law, a transcript of His holy character. When the voice of God roars from Zion, the law goes forth, published by the sealed ones, who are the living demonstration of the character of God—the first fruits of the redeemed.

> They shall walk after the LORD [the 144,000 walk after the Lord, following the Lamb wherever He goes]: he shall roar like a lion: when he shall roar, then the children shall tremble from the west. They shall tremble as a bird out of Egypt, and as a dove out of the land of Assyria: and I will place them in their houses, saith the LORD. (Hosea 11:10, 11)

> The LORD also shall roar out of Zion, and utter his voice from Jerusalem; and the heavens and the earth shall shake: but the LORD will be the hope of his people, and the strength of the children of Israel. (Joel 3:16)

> And he said, The LORD will roar from Zion, and utter his voice from Jerusalem; and the habitations of the shepherds shall mourn, and the top of Carmel shall wither. (Amos 1:2)

> "When God utters His voice, the word that goes out of His mouth will not return to Him void. Why? Because the Spirit of God gives the word unlimited power. The wicked may deny the power; they may initially refuse to recognize it as the voice of God; but the righteous will heed the roar of their Lion-Lamb and "come trembling as a bird" out of spiritual Egypt, Assyria, and Babylon and join the hosts of the Prince."

When God utters His voice, the word that goes out of His mouth will not return to Him void. Why? Because the Spirit of God gives the word unlimited power. The wicked may deny the power; they may initially refuse to recognize it as the voice of God; but the righteous will heed the roar of their Lion-Lamb and "come trembling as a bird" out of spiritual Egypt, Assyria, and Babylon and join the hosts of the Prince. As it is prophesied, "The Lord gave the word: great was the company of those that published it" (Ps. 68:11).

The Gathering Time

In the history of Israel, there are two divisions: the scattering times and the gathering times. The former occur as a result of apostasy and unfaithfulness, while the latter occur as a result of repentance and revival. The focal point of sacred history and all of heaven's energies is on the final revival and gathering of Israel in the end-time fold under one Shepherd. The Father of humanity longs to gather us from the four winds of the earth and establish His kingdom of righteousness and justice among us—a world without end (see Isa. 45:17).

This event brightened the hope of both prophets and apostles. Even with the relative purity of the early Christian church, the apostles still acknowledged they were in a scattering time and the "falling away" had already begun. Almost mournfully, the apostle James addressed his epistle to the churches as "to the twelve tribes that are scattered abroad" (1:1). By contrast, John the beloved was given a vision of the final gathering of these same tribes together with the great unnumbered multitude in Revelation 7. It's this final gathering of Israel that Ezekiel's vision portrays in chapters 47 and 48.

Whereas at the beginning of Ezekiel, chapters 1–11, the divine presence reluctantly, agonizingly leaves the old temple desolate and Israel scattered, at the end, in the new temple, we see the people of God liberated from their captivity to sin, and the glory of God returns to them and never departs.

Chapter 9

Revelation's Cleansing of the Sanctuary

Repent ye therefore, and be converted, that your sins may be blotted out, when the times of refreshing shall come from the presence of the Lord.

Acts 3:19

One way of understanding Ezekiel's temple better is by comparing how both this temple and the Levitical tabernacle align with the final atonement of Christ described in Revelation. These parallel descriptions explain each other and shed light on the current, end-time ministry of Christ for us. Below, we'll look first at the main parallels of the Levitical Day of Atonement to the ministry of Christ described in Revelation and then at the parallels between Revelation and Ezekiel's temple.

The Levitical service teaches that there are two stages involved in the purging of our sins: 1) their initial atonement, when we confess our sins and their burden of guilt is removed from us and transferred to the heavenly sanctuary, symbolized by the ancient *daily* service; and 2) the final blotting out of their record by Christ from the heavenly sanctuary, symbolized by the *yearly* Day of Atonement. For a more in-depth explanation, see Appendix A.

Most Christians teach that once a person's sins are confessed, they are removed permanently and thrown into the depths of the sea, never to be remembered again. The Scriptures support that view to a point: They do teach that when we come to Christ confessing our sins, they are blotted from our record, and we stand free and clear of them before God as though we had never sinned. This is wonderfully good news and *central* to the gospel.

Nevertheless, the ancient services also teach that when our record is cleared of sin, they are transferred to heaven's books, where they stay until their final blotting out on the great anti-typical day of atonement. At Pentecost, Peter, full of the Holy Spirit, exhorted his listeners, "Repent ye therefore, and be converted, *that your sins may be blotted out, when the times of refreshing* [the latter rain] *shall come from the presence of the Lord*" (Acts 3:19, emphasis added).

Notice the close connection the apostle makes between the latter rain and the blotting out of sin. He says the refreshing is not optional but essential to our final cleansing. This agrees with the inspired metaphor. In ancient Israel, the latter rain was absolutely essential to ripen the harvest. No latter rain, no harvest. The very purpose of the latter rain is our sealing and atonement by the blotting out of our sin.

Since this is a new thought to some and one that is controverted by others, let's look carefully now at the Levitical Day of Atonement service, comparing it to the passages in Revelation that describe the latter rain and final ministry of Christ to see what the Scriptures teach and what the practical implications are.

> And the LORD said unto Moses, Speak unto Aaron thy brother, that he come not at all times into the holy place within the veil before the mercy seat, which is upon the ark; that he die not: for I will appear in the cloud upon the mercy seat. Thus shall Aaron come into the holy place: with a young bullock for a sin offering, and a ram for a burnt offering. He shall put on the holy linen coat, and he shall have the linen breeches upon his flesh, and shall be girded with a linen girdle, and with the linen miter shall he be attired: these are holy garments; therefore shall he wash his flesh in water, and so put them on. And he shall take of the congregation of the children of Israel two kids of the goats for a sin offering, and one ram for a burnt offering. And Aaron shall offer his bullock of the sin offering, which is for himself, and make an atonement for himself, and for his house (Lev. 16:2–6).

Before Aaron could make atonement for Israel, he was required to first make an atonement for himself and his house. Notice the animal used for his sin offering—a bull. Compare this with the sin offering of the people—a goat.

> And he shall take the two goats, and present them before the LORD at the door of the tabernacle of the congregation. And Aaron shall cast lots upon the two goats; one lot for the LORD, and the other lot for the scapegoat. And Aaron shall bring the goat upon which the LORD'S lot fell, and offer him for a sin offering. But the goat, on which the lot fell to be the scapegoat, shall be presented alive before the LORD, to make an atonement with him, and to let him go for a scapegoat into the wilderness (Lev. 16:7–10).

Two goats were used to atone for the congregation: one for a sin offering to cleanse the sanctuary and the other, the scapegoat, to bear their sins from the sanctuary into the wilderness, a symbol of the desolate earth during the Millennium where the devil is confined in chains until judged and destroyed with the wicked in the lake of fire. (See Rev. 19:20, 20:1–5, and 21:8.)

> And Aaron shall bring the bullock of the sin offering, which is for himself, and shall make an atonement for himself, and for his house, and shall kill the bullock of the sin offering which is for himself: And he shall take a censer full of burning coals of fire from off the altar before the LORD, and his hands full of sweet incense beaten small, and bring it within the vail: And he shall put the incense upon the fire before the LORD, that the cloud of the incense may cover the mercy seat that is upon the testimony, that he die not: And he shall take of the blood of the bullock, and sprinkle it with his finger upon the mercy seat eastward; and before the mercy seat shall he sprinkle of the blood with his finger seven times (Lev. 16:11–14).

The mercy seat represented the throne of God which rests on His law, the Ten Commandments, the foundation of His government. Sprinkling the blood seven times on the east facing side of the mercy seat symbolized the blood of Jesus offered for us before the throne which, in the tabernacle, faced east. The tabernacle was laid out so that the people and the officiating priests faced west towards the Holiest during their worship—the opposite of the sun worshiping cults of paganism, which face east towards the rising sun.

> Then shall he kill the goat of the sin offering, that is for the people, and bring his blood within the vail, and do with that blood as he did with the blood of the bullock, and sprinkle it upon the mercy seat,

and before the mercy seat: And he shall make an atonement for the holy place, because of the uncleanness of the children of Israel, and because of their transgressions in all their sins: and so shall he do for the tabernacle of the congregation, that remaineth among them in the midst of their uncleanness. And there shall be no man in the tabernacle of the congregation when he goeth in to make an atonement in the holy place, until he come out, and have made an atonement for himself, and for his household, and for all the congregation of Israel (Lev. 16:15–17).

Interestingly, the atonement in the Most Holy Place atoned for both apartments. This agrees with the facts that 1) the veil between them was drawn aside, indicating that the work of the High Priest extended to both apartments and 2) no one was permitted in either apartment except the High Priest, further confirming that the Holy Place was also cleansed by his atonement.

And he shall go out unto the altar that is before the LORD, and make an atonement for it; and shall take of the blood of the bullock, and of the blood of the goat, and put it upon the horns of the altar round about. And he shall sprinkle of the blood upon it with his finger seven times, and cleanse it, and hallow it from the uncleanness of the children of Israel. And when he hath made an end of reconciling the holy place, and the tabernacle of the congregation, and the altar, he shall bring the live goat: And Aaron shall lay both his hands upon the head of the live goat, and confess over him all the iniquities of the children of Israel, and all their transgressions in all their sins, putting them upon the head of the goat, and shall send him away by the hand of a fit man into the wilderness. (Leviticus 16:18–21)

In the Levitical service, Israel experienced atonement, and the sanctuary was cleansed in the autumn at the close of the growing season on the Day of Atonement, a symbol of the final gospel harvest. During the year, sins had been confessed and transferred to the sanctuary, a symbol of the atonement of Christ in the heavenly sanctuary from the fall of Adam to today. The Day of Atonement pointed forward to the end of the age, when these would be blotted out and the heavenly sanctuary would be cleansed at the refreshing that ripens the final harvest.

In the Levitical service, the annual purging of sin took place in two stages: the first at the mercy seat covering the ark of the covenant containing the broken law, and the second and final stage at the golden altar of incense.

In the initial stage, at the mercy seat, the high priest first atoned for himself and his family with a bull for a sin offering. Next, he atoned for the congregation with a goat for the sins of the people. In both cases, except for the animal, the ritual was identical: The blood, representing the life of the innocent animals, was brought to the mercy seat, a symbol of the throne of God, where it was sprinkled seven times directly above the law contained within the ark, first with the blood of the bull and then with the blood of the goat. The Scriptures state that this perfect, sevenfold cleansing atoned for the entire sanctuary, both the Holy and Most Holy places (see Lev. 16:16).

From this divine illustration, we can see the *yearly* service was the cure or remedy for the *daily* services, which had transferred the sins of the people to the sanctuary. In the same way, at the end of time, as the ministry of Christ comes to a close, there is a final removal and blotting out of previously confessed sins. The atonement of Christ under the refreshing of His Spirit is combined with the trials and tests of last-day events that reveal to God's people what is in their hearts and whether their sins have been truly confessed and forsaken. This ministry of Christ seals the person in a sacred, tender, covenant relationship with God.

During this part of the service, no one was permitted to be in either apartment of the sanctuary other than the high priest (see Lev. 16:17). Except for the tinkling of the bells on the border of the high priest's robe, the sanctuary fell silent. It was a day of judgment, and Israel was quiet and humble before the Lord, dependent on the work of one man.

This period of silence in the ancient sanctuary is prophetic, pointing us forward to those end-time prophecies where the court of heaven convenes, the judgment is set, and the Ancient of Days presides, holding a seven-sealed scroll in His right hand.

> As I looked, thrones were placed, and the Ancient of Days took his seat; his clothing was white as snow, and the hair of his head like pure wool; his throne was fiery flames; its wheels were burning fire. A stream of fire issued and came out from before him; a thousand thousands served him, and ten thousand times ten thousand stood before him; the court sat in judgment, and the books were opened.... I saw in the night visions, and behold, with the clouds of heaven there came one like a son of man, and he came to the Ancient of Days and was presented before him. And to him was given dominion and glory and a kingdom, that all

peoples, nations, and languages should serve him; his dominion is an everlasting dominion, which shall not pass away, and his kingdom one that shall not be destroyed. (Daniel 7:9, 10, 13, 14, ESV)

In John's parallel vision, when the Father takes His place on the throne, scroll in hand, we have a still fuller picture. In this account, once the court is seated, the all-important question is posed: "Who is worthy to take the book and break its seals?" Silence and suspense follow while a universal search is made, but no created being in heaven or earth is found worthy to take the book or even look on it (see Rev. 5:1–3).

John was so distraught by this, he cried bitter tears of anguish. No created being, none of even the most exalted and powerful of the heavenly hosts had come forward to speak or open the book. As it became painfully clear that no one had been found, John's suspense changed to anguish. This was not just a passing indisposition. We're told he "wept much" (verse 4). He understood, in some sense, that the destiny of God's people was trembling in the balance—that humanity was doomed unless these seals were broken and the providence of God was unlocked and fulfilled in the final events of earth's history.

John's anguish evoked the sympathy of one of the twenty-four elders who bid him look up and take heart; the elder assured him that the Lamb had indeed prevailed to break the seals and open the book (see verse 4, 5).

At the elder's bidding, John looks, and the scene has changed: a Lion-Lamb, the Priest-King, is brought near by a heavenly escort to the Ancient of Days and presented before Him (Dan. 7:13; Rev. 5:6). The Lamb takes the scroll from the Father's hand, and as he breaks the first four seals, a voice of thunder summons four horsemen in succession; soon afterward, the Lamb breaks open the remaining three.

Just as on the Day of Atonement, there was a sevenfold blood cleansing of the mercy seat, a symbol of the divine throne, so there are seven seals on the scroll when the Father takes His seat on the throne of judgment. By virtue of the blood of the Lamb, these seals are broken, and the final course of earth's history unfolds before the prophet.

As in the typical service, where no one was permitted within the sanctuary for the duration of its cleansing, so in the antitype, no one except the Lion-Lamb is permitted to read the scroll and break its seals. Only the Son of Man can unlock earth's final events and fully liberate us from the dominion of sin. Only He can inspect and cleanse the sanctuary of our souls of their defilement because only He has been tempted in all points like we are yet fully overcame. He is the one being in all of creation who perfectly, mysteriously combines human nature with the divine. He alone holds the remedy for our sin: His own blood, which has infinite power to acquit, cleanse, and transform our souls.

With the deepest interest, all heaven beholds, in silent wonder, this mediatorial work of the Lamb. So far, six seals have been broken. At the seventh and final seal, there is a second, still more profound silence: this time, for the space of about half an hour[19] (see Rev. 8:1). Just as the first pause and silence marked the start of the cleansing of the Holy and Most Holy places, this one marks its completion. After the sevenfold sprinkling of the mercy seat, the high priest exits the Most Holy Place to perform the last stage—the climax of his work: the cleansing of the golden altar.

> As in the typical service, where no one was permitted within the sanctuary for the duration of its cleansing, so in the antitype, no one except the Lion-Lamb is permitted to read the scroll and break its seals. Only the Son of Man can unlock earth's final events and fully liberate us from the dominion of sin.

Cleansing the Golden Altar

The fulfillment of the cleansing depicted in type in Leviticus 16:18–19 is found in Revelation 8. In this scene, after the half hour of silence (see verse 1), Christ approaches the golden altar of incense. Like in the type, He is given much incense—two nail-pierced hands full of His fragrant righteousness—to mingle with our prayers, making them aromatic and beautiful before God (see verse 2–4).

These are the prayers of those who cry and sigh between the porch and the altar for their own sins and those of God's people (see Ezek. 9:4; Joel 2:17). As a tender, attentive Father, the Lord hears those who earnestly intercede with Him for themselves and others. He encourages their perseverance and patience and then answers their petitions with His Spirit and seal.

By the virtue of His blood, Christ imparts the refreshing to them as He casts the fire of His Spirit on the earth, accompanied by "voices, and thunderings, and lightnings, and an earthquake" (Rev. 8:5; see also Ezek. 10:2, 6, 7). Then the first five of the seven trumpets sound in quick succession.

---

[19] This half hour is symbolic. Some believe it can be reckoned in literal time on the day-for-year principle, thus equating to about one week.

Whether these are literal, symbolic, or a combination of both is not easy to say, but they clearly contain symbolic elements. What's clear is their purpose: They are divine warnings—trumpet calls to repentance. They sound globally as Christ completes the cleansing of the golden altar:

- First trumpet: Fiery hail mingled with blood consumes all the grass and a third of the trees of the earth.

- Second trumpet: A giant burning object, the size of a mountain, is thrown into the sea, destroying a third of the ships and sea life.

- Third trumpet: A deadly "star" falls on the springs and rivers of fresh water poisoning a third of them.

- Fourth trumpet: The sun, moon, and stars are struck so that a third of their light is obscured.

- Fifth trumpet: The bottomless pit opens, and locusts emerge that torment unrepentant humanity for five months (see Rev. 8:6–13; 9:1–12).

At the sounding of the sixth trumpet, the cleansing of the golden altar is almost complete. A voice issues from its blood-cleansed horns, releasing the four angels who, until this point, have held back the four winds of strife:

And the sixth angel sounded, *and I heard a voice from the four horns of the golden altar* which is before God, Saying to the sixth angel which had the trumpet, *Loose the four angels which are bound in the great river Euphrates.* And the four angels were loosed. (Revelation 9:13–15, emphasis added)

Just as the seven seals of Revelation are symbolized in Leviticus 16 by the sevenfold cleansing of the mercy seat, the seven trumpets are symbolized by the sevenfold sprinkling of the golden altar. The trumpets are the final call to humanity that announces the closing of Christ's work there. Once the work of blotting out is complete, at the seventh trumpet, great voices in heaven proclaim, "The kingdoms of this world are become the kingdoms of our Lord, and of his Christ; and he shall reign for ever and ever," and the Father announces, "It is done" (11:19; 16:17).

The dominion of sin is at an end. Evil and the devil are vanquished. At last, the sins of God's people are forever blotted out. They are born out of the heavenly sanctuary by Christ and placed on the head of the scapegoat, representing Satan, who is led into the wilderness and then to his destruction in the lake of fire. Probation for humanity has closed, and soon the Son of man appears in the clouds. He puts His sickle to the wheat and gathers every precious grain of it into His garner (see 14:14–16).

The Spring Atonement in Ezekiel's Temple

One of the most notable differences between the Levitical tabernacle and Ezekiel's temple is the latter has quite a different annual atonement service, and this new rite is observed in the spring rather than in the fall. At first glance, Ezekiel's temple seems to do away with the Levitical Day of Atonement, but that is not what is happening.

The biblical principle of repeat and expand is at work: Ezekiel's temple is a window into or expansion of the Day of Atonement. While the Levitical service covers the ministry of Christ for mankind from the fall of Adam to the close of human probation, Ezekiel's temple covers the final phase of Christ's atonement in more detail. It zooms in especially on the latter rain and judgment of the living.

These two are inseparable because the latter rain brings the most powerful, comprehensive revelation of Christ and the truth ever witnessed since the fall of Adam. It is this flood of divine light and glory that calls the world to account. When the truth of God's character is on display in both the words and characters of His people, the Holy Spirit has a clear, unobstructed channel through which to enlighten the world, calling it to repentance and convincing it of sin, righteousness, and judgment (see John 16:8).

In Ezekiel's temple, this is pictured in the new arrangement of furniture, where the golden altar is absent. What's become of it? I suggest it has been cleansed and replaced by the table of shewbread called, in Ezekiel's temple, "the table that is before the Lord." This new altar is located precisely where the golden altar once stood: directly before the throne or mercy seat (see Ezek. 41:22).

In the final phase of His atonement, Christ triumphs in His people. He purifies not only the Holy and Most Holy places and the golden altar, as in the tabernacle, but He also purifies the entire temple, including the bronze altar and the inner court, which is the court of the priests.

When the sons of Levi are purified as foretold in Malachi 3, the first fruits of Christ's atonement appear on Mount Zion in glorious victory with Him on a sea of glass, the great antitype of "the table that is before the Lord" (Ezek. 41:22; see also Rev. 4:6; 14:1–5; 15:2). This sets the wheels of end-time prophecy in irresistible motion that does not stop until the voice of God issues from the throne, saying, "It is done," and the plan of salvation is gloriously complete.

Chapter 10

The Apostles on Our Access to the Holiest

Since 1844, Adventists have taught that this year marks the start of the antitypical day of atonement, when Christ entered the Most Holy Place of the heavenly sanctuary to complete His new covenant work. This view has been rejected by other churches because of passages, especially those in Hebrews, that indicate He entered the Most Holy Place after He rose from the dead. As with all apparent contradictions in Scripture, there is a simple explanation and an underlying harmony.

The atonement of Christ before the Father in heaven is like His sacrifice on the cross: Both acts are foundational, infinite, and eternal. The crucifixion took place at a certain point in time, but it is infinite and timeless: The Lamb was "slain from the foundation of the world" (Rev. 13:8). Whether a person was born before or after the cross, if he or she looks in faith to the Lamb, that person is saved by virtue of that eternal sacrifice.

The prophets and apostles are clear that the blood of animals did not cleanse the conscience of the worshiper; only the Spirit of God mediated by the Son has power to save the soul. The godly men and women of antiquity also understood this. They knew the blood of bulls and goats was a symbol that pointed forward to the true sacrifice: the Lamb of God.

Looking forward to Christ, Job testified, "I know *that* my redeemer liveth, and *that* he shall stand at the latter *day* upon the earth" (Job 19:25).

In the same way the sacrifice of Christ is eternal, His mediatorial work within the Most Holy Place is also timeless and infinite, so whether one lives before or after 1844, if that person looks in faith to the atonement of Christ in the Most Holy Place, it is equally effective.

At the death of Christ, the veil concealing the Holiest from view was torn asunder, and by this, the Holy Spirit taught that the way into the Holiest was now open to all through the "new and living way." Today, we may come boldly to the throne of grace with confidence before God (see Matt. 27:51; Heb. 10:20).

Paul contrasted the blood sacrifices under the two covenants:

> Wherefore when he cometh into the world, he saith, Sacrifice and offering thou wouldest not, but a body hast thou prepared me: In burnt offerings and sacrifices for sin thou hast had no pleasure. Then said I, Lo, I come (in the volume of the book it is written of me,) to do thy will, O God [quoting from Psalm 40:6–8 and 50:8–23]. Above when he said, Sacrifice and offering and burnt offerings and offering for sin thou wouldest not, neither hadst pleasure therein; which are offered by the law; Then said he, Lo, I come to do thy will, O God. He taketh away the first, that he may establish the second. By the which will we are sanctified through the offering of the body of Jesus Christ once for all. And every priest standeth daily ministering and offering oftentimes the same sacrifices, which can never take away sins: But this man, after he had offered one sacrifice for sins for ever, sat down on the right hand of God; From henceforth expecting till his enemies be made his footstool [Ps. 110:1]. For by one offering he hath perfected for ever them that are sanctified. Whereof the Holy Ghost also is a witness to us: for after that he had said before, This is the covenant that I will make with them after those days, saith the Lord, I will put my laws into their hearts, and in their minds will I write them; And their sins and iniquities will I remember no more. [Jer. 31:33, 34]. Now where remission of these is, there is no more offering for sin. Having therefore, brethren, boldness to enter into the holiest by the blood of Jesus, By a new and living way, which he hath consecrated for us, through the veil, that is to say, his flesh; And having an high priest over the house of God; Let us draw near with a true heart in full assurance of faith, having our hearts sprinkled from an evil conscience, and our bodies washed with pure water. (Hebrews 10:6–22)

One reason the above ideas do not sit well with many Jews and Christians is they've been taught that their bloodline, affiliation, rituals, traditions, or some combination thereof saves them. In the case of Adventists, it's more subtle. Some assume, at least subconsciously, that by virtue of being born after 1844, they have special access to the Most Holy Place ministry of Christ.

However, most have never critically examined their assumptions, and many prefer not to do so. Unfortunately, by these views, they alienate themselves from both the gospel and the common bond of union with the righteous of all ages who have gone before us, perfecting holiness in the fear of the Lord (see 2 Cor. 7:1). Joseph Bates, the first of the Millerites to accept the Sabbath, did not do this. He identified himself with the righteous of all ages and taught that the 144,000 were from all generations. This view is closer to the Scriptures, but the exact composition of the 144,000 is a minor point.

The main point is that religious people need to humbly acknowledge their error. Ezekiel's temple teaches us that, from the fall of Adam until today, Israel--whether national or spiritual--has open doors and continuous access to the very throne room of God. If we would solidly grasp this by faith and come boldly to the throne of grace, like the patriarchs, prophets, and early church did, we would be helped, divisions between parties, races, and sects would be set aside, and we would be united before the throne and a power in the world.

I leave the reader with the following two sample quotes as primers for further, more in-depth personal study of the topic. Notice in the emphasized part of the second quotation that the prophet pointed to the infinite, eternal sacrifice of Christ, linking it to our unlimited access to the throne of God. This is a topic worthy of close attention and one that should be an anchor for the soul so we are solidly grounded in what we believe.

> When Christ cried, "It is finished," God's unseen hand rent the strong fabric composing the veil of the Temple from top to bottom. *The way into the Holiest of all was made manifest. God bowed His head satisfied.* Now His justice and mercy could blend. He could be just, and yet the justifier of all who should believe on Christ. He looked upon the victim expiring on the cross, and said, "It is finished. The human race shall have another trial." The redemption price was paid, and Satan fell like lightning from heaven. (White, *Manuscript Releases*, vol. 12, p. 409, emphasis added)

> At the moment that the expiring Saviour exclaimed, "It is finished," an unseen hand rent the veil of the Temple from the top to the bottom. Thus God said, "I can no longer reveal My presence in the Most Holy Place." Type had met antitype in the death of God's Son. *The Lamb of God, slain from the foundation of the world, is dead. The way into the Holiest of all is laid open. A new and living way, which has no veil between, is offered*

to all. From henceforth all may walk in this way. No longer need sinful, sorrowing humanity await the coming of the high priest. It was as if a living voice had spoken to the worshipers: There is now an end to all sacrifices and offerings. The Son of God has come according to His word, "Lo, I come: in the volume of the book it is written of Me, I delight to do thy will, O My God" [Psalm 40:8]. "Behold the lamb of God, which taketh away the sin of the world" [Joh 1:29]. (White, *Manuscript Releases*, vol. 12, p. 416, emphasis added)

Chapter 11

The Daily Worship Services Compared

In the Levitical tabernacle, a daily national worship service was performed each morning and evening. Inspiration underscores the importance of this service, calling it the "continual burnt offering," a symbol of uninterrupted intercession and communion between God and His people.

> Now this is what you shall offer on the altar: Two lambs of the first year, day by day continually. One lamb you shall offer in the morning and the other lamb you shall offer at twilight.... *This shall be a continual burnt offering throughout your generation at the door of the Tabernacle of Meeting before the Lord, where I will meet you to speak with you. And there I will meet with the children of Israel and the tabernacle shall be sanctified by my glory....* I will dwell among the children of Israel and will be their God; And they shall know that I am the Lord their God who brought them up out of the land of Egypt that I may dwell among them. I am the Lord their God. (Exodus 29:38, 39, 42, 43, 45, 46, emphasis added)

As stated above, the daily Levitical offering consisted of two lambs: one for the morning and one for the evening service. At both services, incense was also offered on the golden altar before the Holiest, and at the same time, the seven-branched lampstand was fueled and trimmed (see Exod. 30:7). All three acts of worship—the offering of the lamb, the burning of incense, and the tending of the lampstand—were repeated twice daily: once in the morning, when the doors of the temple were opened; and once just before sundown, when the doors of the temple were shut.

In contrast to the Levitical service, in Ezekiel's temple, the daily service is conducted once only, at dawn, because unlike the tabernacle or the first and second temples, this temple is never shut. It has no closing service. Those who minister there, like the redeemed in Revelation, "serve God day and night in his temple" (7:15).

This change again underscores the unlimited, 24/7 access of new covenant Israel to the throne of God. It affirms the invitation to come boldly into God's direct presence and stand before Him in the name of our Prince. However, it also has a warning message for the Christian world.

The suspension of the evening service in Ezekiel's temple portends a judgment hour in the church when there is no longer a sacrifice for those who have not cherished the light of truth. In the parable of Christ, when the midnight cry is sounding, "Behold the bridegroom cometh, go ye out to meet him," and the latter rain is being poured out, the five unwise virgins discover they are out of oil. There is no evening sacrifice to atone for their failure to heed the Spirit's promptings, and they are left in the dark, shut out of the wedding supper (see Matt. 25:1–13).

> "The suspension of the evening service in Ezekiel's temple portends a judgment hour in the church when there is no longer a sacrifice for those who have not cherished the light of truth."

Flour, Oil, and Wine

In the daily service of Ezekiel's temple, not only has the frequency of the daily worship changed; the accompanying offerings have as well. While a young male lamb is offered in both cases, the amounts of flour, oil, and wine that accompany the burnt offering have changed. In the Levitical service, the lamb is accompanied by one-tenth of an ephah of fine flour (about one gallon or four liters) mixed with one-fourth of a hin of olive oil (about one quart or liter) and a separate wine libation of the same amount; in Ezekiel's temple, the flour and oil offerings are bumped up to one-sixth of an ephah and one-third of a hin—a substantial increase of 67% and 33%, respectively; but no wine libation is made (compare Numbers 28:1–8 with Ezekiel 46:13–15). What do these changes mean?

In Scripture, oil is a symbol of the Holy Spirit (see Zech. 4:1–6). An increase in the oil represents an increase in the gifts of the Spirit under the new covenant and latter rain. I suggest the increase in the flour represents a corresponding increase in the love and good works of the body of Christ.

The absence of wine is intriguing. It appears to be symbolic of the promise of Christ to not drink of the fruit of the vine until He drinks it new with us in His kingdom. Our Prince is on a wine fast as He waits for us, His bride, at His marriage supper.

Chapter 12

The Daily of Daniel

Yea, he magnified himself even to the prince of the host, and by him the daily ~~sacrifice~~ was taken away, and the place of his sanctuary was cast down. And an host was given him against the daily ~~sacrifice~~ by reason of transgression, and it cast down the truth to the ground; and it practised, and prospered. Then I heard one saint speaking, and another saint said unto that certain saint which spake, How long shall be the vision concerning the daily ~~sacrifice~~, and the transgression of desolation, to give both the sanctuary and the host to be trodden under foot?

...And from the time that the daily ~~sacrifice~~ shall be taken away, and the abomination that maketh desolate set up, there shall be a thousand two hundred and ninety days.

Daniel 8:11–13, 12:11

In the above texts, the word "sacrifice," which appears in the King James Version, has been crossed out because it is not in the Hebrew manuscripts but was added by the translators who were attempting to clarify the meaning. The topic of the "daily" or "continual" has been debated within Adventism for more than a century, sometimes too vehemently. We've been advised by the prophet not to do this or make it a test of faith.

Nevertheless, that doesn't mean the topic is inconsequential. It's importance was underscored by Christ. The "daily" is directly connected to the prophecy of Daniel regarding the abomination of desolation Christ admonished the church to both read and understand (see Matt. 24:15). The removing of the daily is caused by this abomination, so we would be well advised to heed Christ's warning and study this topic carefully and prayerfully.

In Daniel 7 and 8, the little horn is a blasphemous power that wars against God and His people. It creates the abomination that removes the daily—an attempted blow at the Prince of the covenant. Historically, by the decree of the Roman emperor Justinian in AD 538, the pope of Rome became the custodian of conscience for the Western Roman Empire, replacing both the false priesthood of paganism and the true priesthood of Christ. The papacy ruled the great majority of the Christian world for the next 1,260 years, until it was deposed by Napoleon in 1798.

How was the daily removed? Rather than yielding to the claims of Christ as the Mediator between God and humanity, Justinian, ostensibly a Christian, invested an apostate church with the prerogatives of God in matters of conscience, making the pope the corrector of heretics. Justinian politically allied himself with complicit church leaders to remove the wall of separation between church and state, making the man of sin the custodian of conscience for the Western Empire.

The removal of the daily in our time therefore constitutes the removal of Christ and His Word as the true custodian of conscience and the ideological triumph of the harlot, "Mystery, Babylon the Great."

However, the Scriptures unmask this victory and the mystery of the harlot for what they are. The victory of the whore is actually the victory of paganism because the wine of her intoxicating false doctrines is paganism and spiritualism baptized.

Many sincere Christians and Jews, especially those in the holiness movement or attracted to Kabbalah, are at risk of not discerning between true and false manifestations of the Spirit because they make their feelings and opinions their criteria. Those who are less mystical and emotional put more weight on the traditions of their sects and clergy or the norms of the community, rather than testing all doctrines by the Word of God.

Babylonian deception only flourishes when humanism, passion, and tradition are placed above the Word. The little horn attempts to remove the daily and thinks to change times and laws (see Dan. 7:25; 8:11–14). As we've seen, it has and will especially attack the seventh commandment, which protects marriage and the family, and the fourth commandment, which protects the sacredness of the seventh-day Sabbath.

In the prophecies, we're told the harlot Babylon, another symbol of the little horn, in the last days becomes "a dwelling place for demons, a haunt for every unclean spirit, a haunt for every unclean bird, a haunt for every unclean and detestable beast. For all nations have drunk the wine of the passion of her sexual immorality" (Rev. 18:2, 3, ESV). She attacks the commandments with apparently great success, slaying the two witnesses in the streets of Sodom, the city that especially tramples the seventh commandment, and Egypt, the city that tramples the fourth[20] (see Rev. 11:7–13).

Additionally, the little horn, Babylon, does more: It even "shall stand up against the Prince of princes, but shall be broken without hand" (Dan. 8:25). The horn is broken because when it stands up to attack and annihilate God's people with cruel, oppressive laws, Michael stands up for them.

This transition from grace to wrath is foretold in the acted prophecy of Zechariah. God instructed him to become a shepherd of the flock "doomed for slaughter." Under divine inspiration, Zechariah took two shepherd's rods, naming one "Favor" or "Beauty" and the other "Unity" or "Bands," and began his work. In one month, he cut off three unprofitable shepherds. Then he quit his position, announcing to his flock:

> "I will not be your shepherd. What is to die, let it die. What is to be destroyed, let it be destroyed. And let those who are left devour the flesh of one another." And I took my staff Favor, and I broke it, annulling the covenant that I had made with all the peoples. (Zechariah 11:9, 10, ESV)

In breaking the staffs of Favor and Unity, Zechariah, in symbol, announced a transition in God's dealings with spiritual Israel at the end of time. There will come a time when those who have claimed to be the children of God, whether Jews or Gentiles, will be separated. The brotherhood between spiritual and nominal Israel will be annulled.

The change in the holy services points us to that time when the ministry of Christ for the sons of darkness is suspended. When apostate Christianity and Judaism sets up its own standard of righteousness and, through the state, enforces laws that compel the conscience, the covenant ministry of the Prince ceases for that body.

Then there is no longer a sacrifice for those who have not cherished the light of truth and the oil of the Spirit. In the wedding parable of Christ, while the midnight cry is sounding, "Behold the bridegroom cometh, go ye out to meet him," and the latter rain is being poured out, while hundreds of thousands are taking their stand for truth, those represented by the

---

[20] Pagan Rome's veneration of the sun god Sol and its naming of the first day of the week after Sol, Sunday, was integrated into Roman Catholicism after the death of the apostles. Rome's pagan veneration can be traced back to the old kingdom of Egypt (2800 BC) and its cult of the sun god, Ra, the greatest god of Egypt, said to be progenitor of the royal line. From there, it can be traced to Nimrod, founder of Babel and chief post-flood rebel.

five unwise virgins are found destitute of the Spirit. There is no longer a evening sacrifice to atone for their failure to heed the Spirit's promptings. Without the evening sacrifice, they are left in the dark and shut out of the wedding supper.

Nevertheless, thankfully, in contrast to the foolish virgins, in Ezekiel's temple, the doors are not shut day or night. They are forever open to God's people and the sons of Zadok.

God, living in the eternal present, has pronounced His redemptive work finished:

And He said to me, "It is done! I am the Alpha and the Omega, the Beginning and the End. I will give of the fountain of the water of life freely to him who thirsts. He who overcomes shall inherit all things, and I will be His God and he shall be my son." (Revelation 21:6, 7, NKJV)

Our salvation is sure. Let's believe God that it is already an accomplished fact.

***

All the powers that hell can muster will not unseat our Prince from His throne. Christ, as a man, has triumphed for us already, and before long, He will cast the beast and dragon into the lake of fire. Christ will be universally, eternally enthroned in the hearts of His people.

Chapter 13

The Sabbath in Ezekiel's Temple

Earlier, I compared the daily burnt offerings of both temples and noted that in the Levitical service, the offering consisted of two male lambs together with their flour, oil, and wine portions.

In the Levitical service, the prescribed Sabbath burnt offering is identical to the daily burnt offering: two lambs, one offered at dawn and the other, just before sunset, together with the prescribed flour offerings and wine libations (see Num. 28:9, 10). The effect of these provisions is that under Levitical law, the Sabbath is celebrated with essentially a double daily offering; it is doubly blessed.

Now recall that in Ezekiel's temple, the daily offering is one lamb only, offered in the morning because this temple is open around the clock, day and night. Furthermore, when it comes to the Sabbath offering, it is remarkably different from that of the Levitical model. Instead of mirroring the morning offering—one male yearling lamb—the Sabbath burnt offering is composed of a ram and *six* lambs, together with their prescribed flour offerings, which, in the case of the ram, is a full ephah of flour—six times the amount offered with each lamb (see Ezek. 46:4). Therefore, in Ezekiel's model, the Sabbath blessing is not merely doubled; it is multiplied.

Curiously, unlike the daily burnt offering, for the Sabbath burnt offering, the amount of flour for each of the six lambs is not prescribed. Instead, the amount is left to the discretion of the Prince according to his ability and desire (see verse 5). The lower limit would likely not be less than the prescribed amount for lambs (normally one sixth of an ephah in Ezekiel's temple), but the upper amount is limited only by the bounty of the Prince. Similarly, there is no limit to the positive influence of the person who becomes a co-laborer with Christ. The limitless resources of heaven are at His command to bless others.

Now, regarding the oil, a symbol of the Spirit, the rule is this: Whatever the Prince chooses to give as a gift of flour, the oil is to be in the ratio of 10:1—that is, one hin of oil to one ephah of flour[21] (see 45:11).

One of the most remarkable changes in Ezekiel's temple is the people have special access to the inner court via the eastern gate *and* special access to the Prince on this sacred day (see 46:1–12; see also the graphic layout of the temple below). And this makes sense. A multiplying of the Sabbath blessings brings a corresponding blossoming and growth of our bond with the Prince.

On the Sabbath, the Prince personally accompanies the people inside the eastern gate and worships there with them. Both people and Prince worship in the inner court by this gate, joining in the hymns led by the choirs of the priests that stand to their right and left, lifting their voices in beautiful anthems of praise.

When their worship is complete, the people are to exit from the court by the same eastern gate (see also Appendix E for a list comparing all the various corporate offerings of the Levitical tabernacle with Ezekiel's temple).

---

[21] The hin is a liquid measure that is not defined in Scripture, but the volume is inferred in that it appears to be the liquid equivalent of the dry omer, which is defined as one-tenth of an ephah (about one gallon). An ephah is about one bushel (about nine American gallons)—a substantial amount.

Layout of Ezekiel's Temple

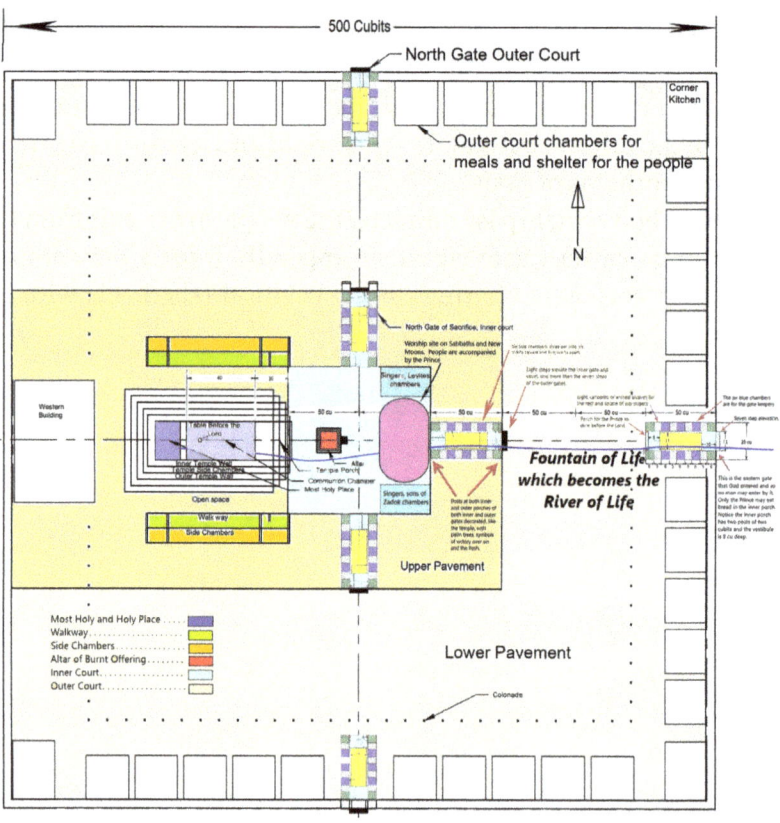

To view this chart at a higher resolution, go to: https://1ref.us/mset6

Chapter 14

The New Moons in Ezekiel's Temple

Among the most notable changes to the order of service in Ezekiel's temple from the Levitical model is the celebration of the new moons. Western nations have adopted the Gregorian calendar, a Roman Catholic calendar, and with that acceptance, we in the West have assumed that the phases of the moon are inconsequential.[22]

However, in the divinely prescribed calendar, the lunar phases are a basic unit of the measurement of time. A look at the Hebrew calendar shows that most of Israel's corporate worship, except for the daily and Sabbath services, are marked by the lunar phases, which are regularly adjusted to synchronize with the seasons.

In the biblical calendar, a month is measured from new moon to new moon. A new moon in Scripture occurs just after the lunar conjunction. Under Levitical law, the new moon was celebrated by a burnt offering identical to that of the seven-day Feast of Unleavened Bread: two bulls, one ram, and seven lambs, together with their corresponding grain offerings and wine libations, as well as a goat for a sin offering (see Num. 28:11–15).

The Levitical new moon, like most of the feast days, was not a Sabbath. There was no prohibition against work. In Ezekiel's temple, the new moon is also not a Sabbath. Its celebration in Ezekiel's temple is still prescribed, but with two notable differences: First, the composition of the burnt offering has changed. Unlike the Levitical model, where the burnt

---

[22] This is not to say the new moons must be celebrated by the church. According to the first church council in Acts 15, they are optional. However, in order to grasp the meaning of the sanctuary and its prophetic significance, we need to understand the operation of the biblical calendar.

offering mirrors the spring feast offerings, in Ezekiel's model, it is similar to the Sabbaths: one bull, one ram, and six lambs, with grain offerings corresponding to Ezekiel's specifications, and like in the other feasts, no wine libation is offered. The second difference is bold—even startling: Unlike in the Levitical service, there is no goat for a national sin offering. We'll come back to this.

The key concept of the Hebrew month is redemption and renewal. While the Sabbath points to the Creator who made the heavens and earth in six days, the new moon points to God as the redeemer of Israel. As the womb of a woman is renewed monthly, the fresh appearance of the new moon that marks the start of the lunar cycle symbolizes the rebirth and regeneration of the twelve tribes, one for each month of the year.

> The key concept of the Hebrew month is redemption and renewal. While the Sabbath points to the Creator who made the heavens and earth in six days, the new moon points to God as the redeemer of Israel. As the womb of a woman is renewed monthly, the fresh appearance of the new moon that marks the start of the lunar cycle symbolizes the rebirth and regeneration of the twelve tribes, one for each month of the year.

This is a clue as to why the weekly Sabbath and monthly new moon burnt offerings in Ezekiel's temple are so similar; these two are the basic elements of the yearly cycle; and both point to God as our Creator and Redeemer. Taken together, the biblical weekly and lunar cycles define the days of the year.

We previously saw that Ezekiel's temple points us to the gathering and reestablishment of Israel. Anciently, it seems that each of the tribes was associated with a particular month. When King Saul, a Benjamite, was celebrating a certain new moon, he planned to use the occasion to slay his son-in-law David. As a member of his family and court, David was obligated to attend this important service, which was celebrated for two days (see 1 Sam. 20:18–30).

Some years later, during David's reign, he organized the national administration of Israel into twelve courses of 24,000 men who served the king and nation for one month on twelve-month rotations (see 1 Chron. 27). Notice that 24,000 is double 12,000, the number of each tribe of the 144,000.

A similar arrangement of government apparently will continue even in the New Jerusalem. This city and divine capitol of the new earth has twelve massive gates of pearl, each inscribed with the name of a tribe. The tree of life also bears twelve kinds of fruit—a different one each month. And the leaves of the tree are for the healing of the tribes or nations[23] (see Rev. 22:2). Isaiah indicates that in the new earth, we will worship from Sabbath to Sabbath and from one new moon to the next (see 66:23).

We saw that the 144,000 are overcomers who are without fault before the throne. To help us grasp this by faith, the sin offering associated with the new moons is suspended in Ezekiel's temple, reassuring us that the bride of Christ will indeed overcome by the blood of the Lamb.

In exchange for the drab garments of her own righteousness, the church, in Revelation 12, is clothed with the sun and adorned with a crown of twelve stars, symbolic of the victory of each of her tribes. And she has been renewed: The full moon shining in its strength, as it does in Jerusalem during her sacred feasts, is under her feet.

> *And there appeared a great wonder in heaven; a woman clothed with the sun, and the moon under her feet, and upon her head a crown of twelve stars.*
>
> Revelation 12:1

> *The Spirit and the bride say,*
> *"Come!"*
>
> Revelation 22:17

---

[23] The word "nations" in the King James Version can be translated in a number of ways. The closest English phrase is "ethnic groups." *Strongs Concordance* indicates that "tribe" is a primary root meaning.

Chapter 15

The Gates

The Eastern Gates

Then he led me to the gate, the gate facing east. And behold, the glory of the God of Israel was coming from the east. And the sound of his coming was like the sound of many waters, and the earth shone with his glory. And I fell on my face. As the glory of the LORD entered the temple by the gate facing east, the Spirit lifted me up and brought me into the inner court; and behold, the glory of the LORD filled the temple.

Ezekiel 43:1–5, ESV

The Sabbaths and new moons of Ezekiel's temple have been divinely linked together in two ways: 1) the burnt offerings are similar—a ram and six lambs for the Sabbath and a bull, a ram, and six lambs for the new moons; and 2) they share the same rules of temple access and worship. The worship on both occasions takes place in the same area of the inner court, accessed via the same gate: exclusively, the eastern inner gate.

Recall that in Ezekiel's temple, there are two eastern gates laid out in a straight line with the elements of the sanctuary. From east to west, these structures are: first, the eastern gate of the outer court, then the eastern gate of the inner court, followed by the bronze altar, the Holy Place, the "table before the Lord," and finally, the Most Holy Place throne room, which is the path the divine glory followed when the Lord returned to the temple (see Appendix C for a map of the layout).

Now, regarding the eastern gate of the *outer* court, the rule of Ezekiel's temple is that because the glory of God returned by that gate, no person may enter the sanctuary through it. Only the Prince himself may eat bread in its vestibule before the Lord because he is the only One who combines divinity with humanity. As the God-Man, the Prince himself is *the* way.

When the Prince is finished with his fellowship meal with the Father, he is to go out the way in which he came; that is, he does not exit the holy precincts but returns back into the courts of the sanctuary. Like the Lord who abides over the cherubim, the Prince has sat down with the Father on His throne. This is his house, palace, and fort. When he reenters the court, then the doors of the inner vestibule of the gate are shut behind him (see Ezek. 44:1–3).

In contrast to the outer eastern gate, on the Sabbaths and new moons, the worshipers are to enter the inner court by way of the *inner* eastern gate, but always accompanied by their Prince. On these days, the gate is to remain open until evening, confirming the entire day is holy[24] (see 46:1–3).

The North and South Gates and Access to the Inner Court

This rule of access on the Sabbaths and new moons is in contrast to the spring and fall feasts, when the worshipers are to approach God through either the north or south gates, again accompanied by their Prince, then continue straight forward and exit by the opposite gate (see verse 9–11).

What does this mean? One lesson is that the worshipers are to go straight forward in the work of sanctification and not retrace their steps. All encounters with God elevate the souls of the worshipers, bringing them blessings, provided they move forward in faith. The saints of God progress from strength to strength by the power of the Spirit working in them. "They go from strength to strength, *every one of them* in Zion appeareth before God" (Ps. 84:7).

The Gate of Sacrifice

In the Levitical temple, the animal sacrifices were slaughtered within the inner court by the bronze altar. In contrast, in Ezekiel's temple, all offerings are slaughtered at the north gate to the inner court, not in the inner court

---

[24] These days are holy in the sense that they are holy appointments. All feast days are holy in this sense, whether or not work was permitted on certain ones.

itself (see Ezek. 40:38–43). This change is related to the following rules of dress and access to the holy altars, at which we'll look now.

One of the main purposes of Ezekiel's vision is to encourage us to be among the number of those who spiritually serve God day and night in His temple like the prophetess Anna (see Luke 2:36) and the Zadokite priesthood. The rules—1) only the order of Zadok has continuous access to the altar of the inner court and the "table before the Lord" and 2) the Zadokites are barred from wearing their holy garments outside the inner court so they do not "sanctify the people with their garments"—are intended to create an ardent desire on our part to be entrusted with such important, sacred responsibilities and come into such close fellowship with our God.

The rules of dress are as follows:

But the priests the Levites, the sons of Zadok, that kept the charge of my sanctuary when the children of Israel went astray from me, they shall come near to me to minister unto me, and they shall stand before me to offer unto me the fat and the blood, saith the Lord GOD: *They shall enter into my sanctuary, and they shall come near to my table, to minister unto me, and they shall keep my charge.* And it shall come to pass, that when they enter in at the gates of the inner court, they shall be clothed with linen garments; and no wool shall come upon them, whiles they minister in the gates of the inner court, and within. They shall have linen bonnets upon their heads, and shall have linen breeches upon their loins; they shall not gird themselves with any thing that causeth sweat. *And when they go forth into the utter court, even into the utter court to the people, they shall put off their garments wherein they ministered, and lay them in the holy chambers, and they shall put on other garments; and they shall not sanctify the people with their garments.* (Ezekiel 44:15–19, emphasis added)

This arrangement shows that unreserved access to the inner courts is limited to the royal priesthood who honor and uphold the law of God. The sons of Zadok, like the 144,000, are clothed in spotless white linen garments, which can't be given to those who are not cleansed and ordained for this work (see Exod. 39:27–29; Lev. 16:4).

Another important purpose of the rules is to warn against spiritual infidelity. Although God is merciful and will forgive those who repent, there are still consequences:

And the Levites that are gone away far from me, when Israel went astray, which went astray away from me after their idols; they shall even bear their iniquity. Yet they shall be ministers in my sanctuary, *having* charge at the gates of the house, and ministering to the house: they shall slay the burnt offering and the sacrifice for the people, and they shall stand before them to minister unto them. Because they ministered unto them before their idols, and caused the house of Israel to fall into iniquity; therefore have I lifted up mine hand against them, saith the Lord GOD, and they shall bear their iniquity. And they shall not come near unto me, to do the office of a priest unto me, nor to come near to any of my holy things, in the most holy *place:* but they shall bear their shame, and their abominations which they have committed. But I will make them keepers of the charge of the house, for all the service thereof, and for all that shall be done therein. (Ezekiel 44:10–14)

We saw previously how in Ezekiel's temple, the Prince is to accompany the people on all the sacred appointments. The blood of the sacrifices is carried on these occasions by the priests from the north gate into the inner court, to the sons of Zadok at the bronze altar. The worshipers, accompanied by the Prince, follow the priests who entered the inner court by virtue of the blood. The sons of Zadok, in turn, receive the blood and apply it to the altar and burn the fat and flesh on it. The people cannot venture into the inner court during unappointed times or on their own without their Prince; and neither can we venture into the presence of the Father except in His appointed ways, always accompanied by the blood and merits of His Son.

Chapter 16

What Days Are Holy?

This brings us to a set of questions: What days on our calendar are holy? Are we to keep these feasts? Catholicism has multiplied its sacred rites and festivals, combining pagan and Christian traditions. Protestantism continues to observe about a quarter-to-a-half of these, depending on the denomination, but what days does the Bible itself say are holy?

The foundational holy day of Scripture is found in the fourth commandment: the seventh-day Sabbath. The seventh and last day of the week is uniquely hallowed, enshrined at the heart of the Ten Commandments, and written by the finger of God in stone. In contrast to the Sabbath, the feasts and new moons are not required. This question was decisively settled at the first church council (see Acts 15).

While observance of the feasts and new moons are not required, they are still very important prophetically and spiritually. As part of the sanctuary service, they illuminate the course of human history, from Eden until the close of time, the plan of redemption, and the priesthood of Jesus Christ.

We are living in this time when our High Priest is ratifying the new covenant in us, so we need to understand how God and Christ are working together to sanctify and seal us in order to cooperate fully with Them. The sanctification of spiritual Israel in God's appointed way is *the* lesson of Ezekiel's temple. As we have seen, that lesson is summarized by the Lord Himself for us in these words: "This is the law of the house; Upon the top of the mountain the whole limit thereof round about shall be most holy. *Behold, this is the law of the house*" (Ezek. 43:12, emphasis added).

Holy Days and Gateways

Returning to the treatment of the Sabbaths and new moons in Ezekiel's temple, why are they unique in allowing Israel access to the very door by which the great glory of God entered?

From antiquity, the Sabbath has been a sign of the creative and redemptive work of God (see Exod. 20:8–11; Deut. 5:12–15). The Sabbath's elevation in Ezekiel's temple points to the Sabbath in the end times as a test of faith for the world. Those who humble themselves and honor the law of God will be sanctified through their willing submission to His revealed will. The Sabbath therefore becomes a testing truth—a gateway. Only those who acknowledge its validity as the sign of God's creative and redemptive power will have access to the inner court of the priests.

In the same way the Sabbath is the visible symbol of our standing before God, the new moons open to us the door of prophetic interpretation. By acknowledging the divine lunar-solar calendar of Scripture and its template for the interpretation of sacred history, we accept the tools inspiration gives to help us understand this history and the apocalyptic prophecies. The augmented new moon worship service of Ezekiel's temple, where the Prince accompanies the worshipers on the twelve new moons of the year, symbolizes the remnant church: the pure and lovely bride, clothed with the sun, and endowed with the testimony of Jesus, which is the Spirit of prophecy.

> Those who humble themselves and honor the law of God will be sanctified through their willing submission to His revealed will. The Sabbath therefore becomes a testing truth—a gateway. Only those who acknowledge its validity as the sign of God's creative and redemptive power will have access to the inner court of the priests.

The claim that our understanding of the Hebrew calendar and its lunar cycle will take on a more prominent role in the remnant church is a new idea to many. Let me add here, though, that I don't believe it is or will be a test of faith. Nevertheless, the fact that Isaiah informs us we'll be worshiping God in the new earth from Sabbath to Sabbath and one new moon to the next evinces the enduring importance of the monthly cycle (see 66:22, 23).

While the new moons are not enshrined in the Decalogue as the Sabbath is—thus, they are not a test of faith or a binding sacred holiday—they are still a prophetically important appointment, a gateway to biblical understanding, and one of the few institutions on earth to graduate into eternity.

What Happened to the Missing Levitical Feasts?

And it came to pass in the fourth year of king Darius, *that* the word of the LORD came unto Zechariah in the fourth *day* of the ninth month, *even* in Chisleu; When they had sent unto the house of God Sherezer and Regemmelech, and their men, to pray before the LORD, *And* to speak unto the priests which *were* in the house of the LORD of hosts, and to the prophets, saying, Should I weep in the fifth month, separating myself, as I have done these so many years? Then came the word of the LORD of hosts unto me, saying, Speak unto all the people of the land, and to the priests, saying, When ye fasted and mourned in the fifth and seventh *month*, even those seventy years, did ye at all fast unto me, *even* to me?... Thus speaketh the LORD of hosts, saying, Execute true judgment, and shew mercy and compassions every man to his brother: And oppress not the widow, nor the fatherless, the stranger, nor the poor; and let none of you imagine evil against his brother in your heart.... Thus saith the LORD of hosts; The fast of the fourth *month*, and the fast of the fifth, and the fast of the seventh, and the fast of the tenth, shall be to the house of Judah joy and gladness, and cheerful feasts; therefore love the truth and peace. (Zechariah 7:1–5, 9, 10, 8:19)

During their seventy-year captivity in Babylon, the Jews had observed the anniversary of Jerusalem's destruction with mourning and fasting (see Zech. 7:1–10; Jer. 52:11, 12). They have observed this fast ever since because the two greatest calamities to befall their nation both fell on this day. Six centuries after the destruction of Jerusalem by the Babylonians, on that same day, the Romans destroyed Jerusalem and the temple a second time and decimated the nation, dispersing the Jews for two millennia.

Referring back to Zechariah 7:3, a delegation of the leading Jews went to the prophet to ask, now that they had returned to Jerusalem and were rebuilding the temple, if they should continue to mourn and fast on this day.

The Lord through Zechariah graciously gave more of an answer than that for which they asked. He pointed out the insincerity of their former fasts yet at the same time reassured them that He had taken note of their recent genuine repentance. God said not only was the fast of the fifth month unnecessary, but also their fasts of the fourth, seventh, and tenth months were not required. Then He encouraged and reassured them that if they remained true to Him and justice and righteousness continued to prevail in their land, He would bless them.

This is the same message to God's people today. Modern Jews, the children of Abraham by faith, are not to mourn over their former personal or national calamities but rather rejoice in the mercy of God and show true repentance by loving truth and peace (see Zech 8:19). Jews who continue to fast today in the fifth month would benefit from reexamining this scripture. This is an important example of God adjusting the calendar of His people, turning our days of fasting into days of rejoicing. Let's look now at some other divine changes to the sacred calendar.

In chapters 9 and 19, I cover the reasons why Ezekiel's temple has a spring rather than a fall atonement. To recap, the purpose of the spring week of atonement is to zoom in and expand on the last phase of the antitypical day of atonement and direct our focus to this special time of cleansing in the remnant. This atonement is linked to the 144,000, the first fruits of Christ's mediatorial work, which appear in the spring, just as the first fruits of harvest appeared at this time in Israel.

However, what about the other three feasts that are absent in Ezekiel's temple: the Feast of Trumpets, the Feast of Firstfruits, and the Feast of Weeks (Pentecost)? And why is the Feast of Purim also missing?

As suggested above, the sacred calendar is the template for the interpretation of sacred history, past and future. Applying that principle to the feasts of Ezekiel's temple, since the vision applies to the end times, this temple gives us the template for the final divine appointments of God with humanity. The feasts of Purim, Firstfruits, and Pentecost are not present because they have been fulfilled. They have no end-time application.

Someone will say, 'But in Ezekiel's temple, the Passover, which was fulfilled, is still celebrated.' That is very true. Not only that, but Passover week is celebrated in this temple twice: once in the spring and again in the fall. Why? Because at the end of time, the Lord will shelter His people in His sanctuary for several months from the plagues He sends on spiritual Egypt, Sodom, and Babylon. During these scourges, the firstborn of spiritual Israel, like the firstborn Hebrews on the night of their liberation, are sheltered in God's pavilion, sealed and protected by the blood on its posts.

Finally, why is the Feast of Trumpets missing in Ezekiel's temple since this feast has never been fulfilled? I suggest the reason is it will be fulfilled before Ezekiel's temple vision goes into full effect.

Chapter 17

The Tribal Boundaries Redrawn

Further evidence that Ezekiel's vision is prophetic of the remnant of Israel under the latter rain is that in this vision, the twelve tribes return from captivity, and the land of Israel is *permanently* redistributed among them (Ezek. 47:13–48:35).

By Ezekiel's time, the ten northern tribes had almost completely lost their identity. They had been absorbed and assimilated into the heathen nations where they had been taken captive. With the exception of the Samaritans and some other fragments, the northern tribes became ethnically extinct. Today, there is still a tiny group of Samaritans in Israel, numbering in the hundreds, who claim they are the true worshipers of God and that Mount Gerizim, rather than the Temple Mount, is the true site of worship.

In the time of Christ, the woman of Samaria asserted this to Him (see John 4:20), and modern Samaritans continue to make the same claim. However, this mixed group, while likely sharing some of their ancestry with the ten northern tribes, have lost their tribal identity. In order for the prophecy of Ezekiel's temple to be fulfilled, it requires an awakening of these spiritual tribes to an awareness of their true identity.

These are the same tribes of the early church the apostle James addressed in his epistle. At this time, they were still "scattered abroad" (1:1). Nevertheless, the promise of Ezekiel's temple is that they will be regathered.

In the same vein, Paul tells us that God, in mercy to the Gentiles, has sent blindness upon Israel until the full number of the Gentiles comes in (see Rom. 11:25). Once these are grafted into the stock of Israel, the blindness will be removed and, as prophesied, all of spiritual Israel will be saved. This is illustrated in Ezekiel's vision by the divine reallotment of land among the regathered tribes (see Ezek. 47, 48).

In Ezekiel's vision, the redistribution of the Promised Land is governed by three rules. The first two rules of subdivision are: 1) Joseph has two portions—one for Ephraim and one for Manasseh; and 2) all twelve portions are *equal* (see 47:14). The equality of territory implies an equality of population, which is what we see with the 144,000, where there are 12,000 in each tribe.

The third rule is that all the Gentiles who choose to become part of Israel are given their full inheritance among their respective tribes of domicile. Under this provision, they obtain the same status as does the bloodline of the native-born citizen (see verses 22, 23). This is a wonderful provision of grace because it means those who are grafted into the stock of Israel are not only full citizens of the nation but also full members of their respective tribes.

Recall that in the New Jerusalem, there are 12 gates, each one dedicated to a tribe and named after it. The only way into the city is through one of these gates. In our new home, we may find that access through each gate is reserved for the members of their respective spiritual tribes. If that's the case, at some point, the Lord will reveal each tribal affiliation of every Gentile, possibly when He gives each saint his or her white stone inscribed with a new name (see Rev. 2:17).

The widespread antisemitism that still exists in our world is rooted in jealousy over the Jews who often seem to rise to the top. The pride and air of condescension of some Jews doesn't help matters (It's hard to be humble when your bloodline generally ranks first in everything). However, there's no need for Gentile jealousy. The grace of God invites every nationality to come to the fountain of life, receive its full inheritance among the tribes of Israel, and be blessed along with them.

> So you shall divide this land among you according to the tribes of Israel. You shall allot it as an inheritance for yourselves and for the sojourners who reside among you and have had children among you. They shall be to you as native-born children of Israel. With you they shall be allotted an inheritance among the tribes of Israel. In whatever tribe the sojourner resides, there you shall assign him his inheritance, declares the Lord GOD. (Ezekiel 47:21–23, ESV)

Chapter 18

The Just Shall Live by Faith

I will stand upon my watch, and set me upon the tower, and will watch to see what he will say unto me, and what I shall answer when I am reproved. And the LORD answered me, and said, Write the vision, and make it plain upon tables, that he may run that readeth it. For the vision is yet for an appointed time, but at the end it shall speak, and not lie: though it tarry, wait for it; because it will surely come, it will not tarry. Behold, his soul which is lifted up is not upright in him: but the just shall live by his faith.

Habakkuk 1:1–4

October 31, 2017 marked the 500th anniversary of Martin Luther's bold challenge to Rome: the nailing of his famous 95 Theses to the door of the Wittenberg Chapel—the start of the Protestant Reformation. However, the personal reformation of Luther himself, who had been a very pious monk, occurred a few years earlier, when a voice like thunder changed the course of his life. Ellen White described the bolt that struck Luther during a pilgrimage to Rome:

> By a recent decretal [decree] an indulgence [grant of forgiveness] had been promised by the pope to all who should ascend upon their knees "Pilate's staircase,"[25] said to have been descended by our Saviour on leaving the Roman judgment hall and to have been miraculously conveyed from Jerusalem to Rome. Luther was one day devoutly climbing these steps, when suddenly a voice like thunder seemed to say to him:

---

[25] The same staircase and the same rite of climbing it on one's knees to obtain divine favor continues today (see https://1ref.us/mset5).

"The just shall live by faith." Romans 1:17. He sprang to his feet and hastened from the place in shame and horror. That text never lost its power upon his soul. From that time he saw more clearly than ever before the fallacy of trusting to human works for salvation, and the necessity of constant faith in the merits of Christ. His eyes had been opened, and were never again to be closed, to the delusions of the papacy. When he turned his face from Rome he had turned away also in heart, and from that time the separation grew wider, until he severed all connection with the papal church. (White, *The Great Controversy*, pp. 124, 125)

The text that thundered in Luther's ears from Romans 1:17 was originally declared by the prophet Habakkuk. "The just shall live by his faith" is both the seed and essence of Protestantism. Over 2,300 years later, the same text again became a major source of inspiration for the great awakening of the Millerite movement.

As early as 1842 the direction given in this prophecy to "write the vision, and make it plain upon tables, that he may run that readeth it," had suggested to Charles Fitch the preparation of a prophetic chart to illustrate the visions of Daniel and the Revelation. The publication of this chart was regarded as a fulfillment of the command given by Habakkuk. No one, however, then noticed that an apparent delay in the accomplishment of the vision—a tarrying time—is presented in the same prophecy. After the disappointment, this scripture appeared very significant: "The vision is yet for an appointed time, but at the end it shall speak, and not lie: though it tarry, wait for it; because it will surely come, it will not tarry.... The just shall live by his *faith*." (White, *The Great Controversy*, p. 392)

This text, which has been central to the reform movements of modern times, awaits a final fulfillment in the outpouring of the latter rain. When the ancient prophet is told to write the vision in a way that will make it plain to the common people, could he be referring especially to the obscure temple vision of Ezekiel?

***

So far, we've reviewed several of the features that demonstrate Ezekiel's temple vision is prophetic. Momentarily, we'll continue our investigation comparing the Levitical and prophetic models. Some of the most interesting, persuasive evidence that Ezekiel's temple depicts Israel under the latter rain is contained within these details.

As was mentioned earlier, Ezekiel's temple vision is interspersed with three admonitions to pay careful attention to each detail and relate it faithfully to the people. When God says something once in Scripture, we're to take careful heed because "man does not live by bread alone but by *every* word that proceeds from the mouth of God" (Matt. 4:4; Luke 4:4). Similarly, when God says something *twice*, we know it's doubly important. However, if He says it *three* times, it's triply imperative that we sit up and pay full attention:

> And the man said unto me, Son of man, behold with thine eyes, and hear with thine ears, *and set thine heart upon all that I shall show thee; for to the intent that I might show them unto thee art thou brought hither: declare all that thou seest to the house of Israel.* (Ezekiel 40:4, emphasis added)

> Thou son of man, *show the house to the house of Israel, that they may be ashamed of their iniquities: and let them measure the pattern.* And if they be ashamed of all that they have done, show them the form of the house, and the fashion thereof, and the goings out thereof, and the comings in thereof, and all the forms thereof, and all the ordinances thereof, and all the forms thereof, and all the laws thereof: and write [it] in their sight, that they may keep the whole form thereof, and all the ordinances thereof, and do them. *This is the law of the house; Upon the top of the mountain the whole limit thereof round about shall be most holy. Behold, this is the law of the house.* (Ezekiel 43:10–12, emphasis added)

> And the Lord said unto me, *Son of man, mark well, and behold with thine eyes, and hear with thine ears all that I say unto thee concerning all the ordinances of the house of the Lord, and all the laws thereof; and mark well the entering in of the house, with every going forth of the sanctuary.* And thou shalt say to the rebellious, *even* to the house of Israel, Thus saith the Lord GOD; O ye house of Israel, let it suffice you of all your abominations. (Ezekiel, 44:5, 6, emphasis added)

Significantly, Revelation, which unseals the meaning of the book of Daniel, also contains a threefold injunction to study and understand its message. Notice the similarity of the threefold admonishment:

Blessed is he that readeth, and they that hear the words of this prophecy, and keep those things which are written therein: for the time is at hand. (Revelation 1:3)

Blessed is he that keepeth the sayings of the prophecy of this book.... Seal not the sayings of the prophecy of this book: for the time is at hand. (Revelation 22:7, 11)

For I testify unto every man that heareth the words of the prophecy of this book, If any man shall add unto these things, God shall add unto him the plagues that are written in this book: And if any man shall take away from the words of the book of this prophecy, God shall take away his part out of the book of life, and out of the holy city, and from the things which are written in this book. He which testifieth these things saith, Surely I come quickly. Amen. Even so, come, Lord Jesus. (Revelation 22:18–20)

A true understanding of the messages of Ezekiel, Daniel, and Revelation is critical to the end-time church. Why? These prophecies will impress us with a sense of our sins and deficiencies of character because the vision of John, like that of Ezekiel, points us to the majesty and holiness of God and Christ.

More than this, they will inspire us with faith, love, and confidence in our Prince. John's Apocalypse is a revelation of Jesus Christ. When we behold the God of heaven who sits enthroned above the cherubim and see Him crucified, our fallen, naked condition is exposed, and our great need for the only remedy, the robe of His righteousness, becomes more apparent.

> A true understanding of the messages of Ezekiel, Daniel, and Revelation is critical to the end-time church. Why? These prophecies will impress us with a sense of our sins and deficiencies of character because the vision of John, like that of Ezekiel, points us to the majesty and holiness of God and Christ.

This is the message of repentance given by the angel to Ezekiel: "Thou son of man, show the house to the house of Israel, that they may be ashamed of their iniquities: and let them measure the pattern" (43:10). The pattern is the law of God revealed in the character of Christ, the Prince of the covenant, who today is seeking to write His law and covenant on our hearts (Jer. 31:33, 34).

Will we allow Jesus to do that? More than anything else, is that what we want? Can we say with the psalmist, "I delight to do thy will, O my God; Yea thy law is within my heart" (Ps. 40:8)? Let's thank and praise Him for His mercy and the gracious opportunities He gives us to seek His face, claiming the promise, like Luther did, "The just shall live by his faith."

Chapter 19

The Spring Atonement and Passover

Atonement Week

In chapter 9, I suggested that the yearly atonement service in Ezekiel's temple, which is quite different from the Levitical Day of Atonement, complements the Levitical model, expanding on its meaning. We'll look at it here in more detail.

The atonement service of Ezekiel's temple is in the spring rather than in the fall, starting on the first day of the first month of the Hebrew calendar, which is in late March/early April. Here, the cleansing is not just a one-day service but spans a week, with not one but *two* cleansing services: one on the first day of the month and one on the seventh day.

The specifications of the service are as follows:

Thus saith the Lord GOD; In the first *month*, in the first *day* of the month, thou shalt take a young bullock without blemish, and cleanse the sanctuary: And the priest shall take of the blood of the sin offering, and put *it* upon the posts of the house, and upon the four corners of the settle of the altar, and upon the posts of the gate of the inner court. And so thou shalt do the seventh *day* of the month for every one that erreth, and for *him that is* simple: so shall ye reconcile the house. (Ezekiel 45:18–20)

In Ezekiel's temple, this spring week of atonement is the only provision for its annual cleansing. The purpose of the cleansing is the same as that of the Day of Atonement: to "purify" or "cleanse" the sanctuary and atone for "everyone that erreth." However, in addition to the timing and duration being changed, there are other major differences.

First, in this atonement, the only sin offering is a bull. Unlike the Levitical model, no goat is offered, indicating that God's ideal for Israel is to be realized: The entire nation/church becomes a royal priesthood. This is evident because under the ceremonial law, while a goat is the offering of the common people, a bull is used exclusively for the priesthood (see Lev. 4–9, 16).

Second, in this atonement, different articles are cleansed. In the Levitical model, on the Day of Atonement, the Most Holy Place, Holy Place, and golden altar are cleansed. In contrast, in Ezekiel's week of atonement, the temple as one unit, the bronze altar, and the inner court are cleansed, and this cleansing purifies the whole of the Temple Mount, such that the entire site is "most holy" (see Lev. 16:19, 20; compare with Ezek. 45:19; 43:7–12).

Significantly, the atonement of Ezekiel's temple cleanses exactly the same objects measured by John in Revelation 11. John's task, like Ezekiel's, was to measure the temple. In both cases, the purpose of measuring is to cooperate with the Prince, Christ, who alone can cleanse it.

What about the timing of this atonement? Why spring? I suggest the riddle is solved by two clues: 1) the kinds of sin that are purged and 2) the Passover theme of this temple.

In Ezekiel's temple, the sins that are purged are sins of error or ignorance. Willful sins were previously purged when the bronze altar was cleansed on its horns at the ordination of the sons of Zadok. The only provision in Ezekiel's temple for willful sins is during the dedication of the bronze altar, before the temple goes into operation.

How do we know that? Because in this case, it is specifically stated that the atonement is "for anyone who sins through error or ignorance" (Ezek. 45:20, ESV).

This is yet another divine plea to new covenant Israel to leave off all willful transgression and put our houses in order so we'll be among the wise virgins who have oil in their lamps (the 144,000 are called both virgins and first fruits). These stand before God on Mount Zion during the final reformation awakening accomplished by the angels of Revelation 14 and 18:1–8.

The Passover Theme

Now, regarding the second clue, the Passover theme in Ezekiel's temple, on the first and seventh days of the year, the blood of the atonement bull is applied to the posts of the temple like the blood of the lambs was to the posts of the Hebrews' homes on the night of the first Passover. The theme continues seven days later during the Passover week and is repeated again in the fall feast, which shares an identical liturgy to the spring Passover feast (see Ezek. 45:25). This temple, therefore, is prophetic of the final Passover and deliverance of God's people.

This interpretation is consistent even with current Jewish tradition. According to modern Judaism, the Passover not only commemorates its emancipation from Egypt but also points forward to the return of Elijah and the messianic kingdom. Modern Judaism has this curious and delightful Passover custom: At the start of the festive meal, a member of the household, usually a child, leaves the table, goes to the door of the home, and opens it to welcome Elijah. If Elijah is not there, then the family looks forward to welcoming him the following year.

Scripture agrees with Judaism regarding Elijah's return. For many centuries now, faithful Christians have also waited for it. The Old Testament closes with this promise and warning:

> Behold, I will send you Elijah the prophet before the coming of the great and dreadful day of the LORD: And he shall turn the heart of the fathers to the children, and the heart of the children to their fathers, lest I come and smite the earth with a curse. (Malachi 4:5, 6)

The fulfillment of this prophecy is pictured in Revelation 11. Before the return of Christ, two witnesses appear, who, like Elijah and Moses, have power to do great miracles and smite the earth with plagues. Though these judgments are severe, they are sent in mercy to awaken revival. Scripture and Jewish tradition agree that this future Passover that shields the remnant church from the plagues will be linked to the Elijah message.

Let's look closer now at Ezekiel's Passover, which falls one week after the spring week of atonement. This is the Passover law of Ezekiel's temple:

> In the first month, in the fourteenth day of the month, ye shall have the Passover, a feast of seven days; unleavened bread shall be eaten. *And upon that day shall the Prince prepare for himself and for all the people of the land a bullock for a sin offering.* And seven days of the feast he shall prepare a burnt offering to the Lord, seven bullocks and seven rams daily the seven days; and a kid of the goats daily for a sin offering. (Ezekiel 45:21–23, emphasis added)

The part I emphasized is remarkable for several reasons. First, under the Levitical model, each household sacrificed a lamb on the afternoon of Nisan 14 and kept the feast that evening in Jerusalem. At every Passover, thousands of lambs were sacrificed at the temple, enough to feed every pilgrim family (see Exod. 12:3–27; Lev. 17:3–7; 23:5–8; Num. 28:16–31; 2 Chron. 35:7–13).

In Ezekiel's model, the multitude of lambs has been replaced by a single bull provided by the Prince for Himself and all the people. Recall that the bull is the offering of the priesthood, so again, the lesson is that when Ezekiel's temple takes effect, new covenant Israel becomes a nation of royal priests, ministering under the protecting blood that is on the posts of the sanctuary.

Speaking of the blood, another notable difference between the Levitical Passover and Ezekiel's is that in the latter, the blood of the Passover bull is applied not only to the corners of the bronze altar but also to the door posts of the temple in the same way it was applied a week earlier during the spring atonement.

The text does not specify how the blood of the Passover bull is to be applied because it is specified in the divine instructions regarding the bull of the atonement. Since it is an identical offering, a bull sin offering, it is applied identically to the posts of the temple, the corners of the bronze altar, and the posts of the inner court (see Eze. 45:18–23).

The way the blood is applied here is quite amazing because in doing this, the Lord combines and equates the atonement provisions of Ezekiel's temple with its Passover provisions and vice versa. In Ezekiel's temple, the Passover service and atonement services are based on the same pattern and provision, both on the bull sin offering, which is provided by the Prince.

Furthermore, the Passover/atonement theme is repeated in the fall feast, which is identical to the spring Passover (Ezek. 45:25). In this way the Passover and atonement themes are beautifully combined and permeate the whole cycle of the year. What an awesome God we serve—One who redeems, protects, and shelters us 24/7, every day of the year, with not a day missing!

Speaking prophetically, King David, a type of our Prince, referred to this future Passover/atonement:

> He that dwelleth in the secret place of the most High shall abide under the shadow of the Almighty [The secret place is the sanctuary of divine protection, which shelters God's people by the blood on its posts]. I will say of the LORD, He is my refuge and my fortress: my God; in him will

I trust. Surely he shall deliver thee from the snare of the fowler, and from the noisome pestilence. He shall cover thee with his feathers, and under his wings [the wings of the covering cherubim who stand before God on the mercy seat] shalt thou trust: his truth shall be thy shield and buckler. Thou shalt not be afraid for the terror by night; nor for the arrow that flieth by day; *Nor* for the pestilence *that* walketh in darkness; *nor* for the destruction *that* wasteth at noonday. A thousand shall fall at thy side, and ten thousand at thy right hand; *but* it shall not come nigh thee. Only with thine eyes shalt thou behold and see the reward of the wicked. Because thou hast made the LORD, *which is* my refuge, *even* the most High, thy habitation; There shall no evil befall thee, neither shall any plague come nigh thy dwelling. For he shall give his angels charge over thee, to keep thee in all thy ways. They shall bear thee up in their hands, lest thou dash thy foot against a stone. Thou shalt tread upon the lion and adder: the young lion and the dragon shalt thou trample under feet. Because he hath set his love upon me, therefore will I deliver him: I will set him on high, because he hath known my name. He shall call upon me, and I will answer him: I will be with him in trouble; I will deliver him, and honour him. With long life will I satisfy him, and shew him my salvation. (Psalm 91)

* * *

Final Thought

In the Levitical model, during the year, the horns of the golden altar received the blood of the sin offerings of the priesthood (see Lev. 4). In Ezekiel's temple, this altar has been replaced by the wooden "table that is before the Lord," which receives no blood.

Through the ministry of Christ at the heavenly altar, Israel is admitted into the order of Zadok, the priesthood that ministers directly before the mercy seat. Here, the golden altar having done its work, the priesthood is represented as standing in God's presence twice atoned, on the first and seventh days of the first month, each time with a bull, and each time resting within God's pavilion, sealed with the blood on its posts.

The remnant church in Revelation 12, pictured as the pure woman, meets the particulars of this description. We are told the saints have overcome the dragon, not by the blood of the lamb *alone*, but also "by the word of their testimony; for they loved not their lives unto death" (verse 11). Those who are admitted to the priestly order of Zadok earn their colors through unswerving fidelity to God even in the face of death. Through faith and trust in the blood of the true Passover Lamb, they are covered and delivered.

Chapter 20

Called to the Priesthood

After giving the law at Mount Sinai, the Lord called Moses to meet with Him on the mount to receive the law written by His own finger in stone, as well as additional instructions. God communed with Moses at this time for forty days. This was a major test of faith for Israel, which became restless and discontent. They murmured again, and their faith failed.

On coming down from the mount, Moses, appalled by the debauchery and idolatry of God's people, hurled the tables of stone to the ground, shattering them, to impress on Israel a sense of the magnitude of their sin. He then made the call, "Who is on the Lord's side?" Levi was the only tribe that responded decisively and obeyed the command of God to inflict punishment on those who were still in open rebellion. The men of Levi had not participated in the sin of Israel, and God used them to punish those who continued in open rebellion. Because of their fidelity, Levi was entrusted with the care and services of the sanctuary. The priesthood, in turn, was selected from the tribe of Levi and entrusted to the family of Aaron.

In Ezekiel's temple, the priesthood is still further restricted, and for the same reasons. Of Aaron's line, only the family of Zadok are given the right to officiate in the most holy services. In conferring the highest honors and greatest responsibility on the Zadokites, God cites the infidelity of the other members of the Aaronic priesthood as the reason for their rejection and rewards and commends the family of Zadok for their faithfulness. The remainder of Aaron's descendants are allowed to continue to officiate, but not in the most sacred duties.

God is not being selective or showing favoritism here. The unfaithful ministers are not rejected due to partiality or vindictiveness, but because, like Moses did on the borders of the Promised Land, they have profaned God's name before the congregation and disqualified themselves from this most sacred work.

The primary duties of the priest were to represent God to the people, teach them to distinguish between good and evil, holy and common, and act as arbiters in disputes (see Ezek. 44:23, 24). Failure of the priests to do this anciently is being repeated today in our modern clergy. This not only misrepresents God but also impairs their personal judgment and compromises their credibility.

> **"**
> The primary duties of the priest were to represent God to the people, teach them to distinguish between good and evil, holy and common, and act as arbiters in disputes. Failure of the priests to do this anciently is being repeated today in our modern clergy. This not only misrepresents God but also impairs their personal judgment and compromises their credibility.
> **"**

An almost identical restriction to the Zadokites applied to Solomon's temple. In the case of that temple, half of Aaron's family was rejected, and the family of Zadok was made the officiating order of priests at the commencement of Solomon's reign. At that time, the family of Abiathar, descended from Aaron's son Ithimar, who were guilty of treason towards Solomon, were banished from Jerusalem but allowed to continue in their offices as priests at the city of Anathoth.

From this we can see the family of Zadok takes on a prophetic significance similar to that of David, Solomon, and Melchizedek, all of whom were types of Christ. The Bible says Ithimar's line was rejected and Zadok's was chosen during Solomon's reign due to the failure of Eli, high priest during Samuel's childhood, to correct the abuses of his sons (see 1 Sam. 2:22–36; 1 Kings 1:5–14; 2:26, 27; 4:1, 2).

Before we go on, there are some other spiritual lessons we should not overlook: First, except for blasphemy and rejection of the Holy Spirit, there is forgiveness for every sin we confess and forsake, including spiritual infidelity. However, notwithstanding God's mercy, there can be long-term consequences. As was pointed out above, the pardoned priesthood must "bear their shame" (Ezek. 44:13). The Lord declared: "Because they ministered unto them before their idols, and caused the house of Israel to fall into iniquity; therefore have I lifted up mine hand against them, saith the Lord GOD, and they shall bear their iniquity" (verse 12). In Scripture, there are only a handful of cases where God takes a solemn oath, lifts His hand, and swears by His name. This is one of them.

A second lesson here is that God's dealing with the priesthood—His requirement that His name be consistently upheld and reverenced by His most responsible representatives—is also a clue to the reason for the exclusion of the Gentiles from the inner court of the temple in Revelation 11:1–2. Spiritual Gentiles are those described by Paul as having a form of godliness but denying the power thereof (see 2 Tim. 3:5). They take the name "Christian" or "Jew" but only profane its meaning. In this way, they trample upon the sacrifice and atonement of their Prince.

All believers today are called to the service and priesthood of Christ, but only those who accept the call and comply with the conditions of salvation are admissible to the inner courts of the temple and the priestly service.

Chapter 21

The Cleansing and the First Fruits

This is the law of the house; Upon the top of the mountain the whole limit thereof round about shall be most holy. Behold, this is the law of the house.

Ezekiel 43:12

The above scripture has been quoted already more than once, but I quote it here again to make the point that this is one of the great new covenant promises of the Bible. In the final phase of His atonement, Christ triumphs in His people. He purifies not only the Holy and Most Holy places, as in the Levitical temple, but also the entire temple, including both altars and the inner court, which is the court of the priests.

When the sons of Levi are purified (see Mal. 3), the first fruits of Christ's atonement appear; the 144,000 appear on Mount Zion in glorious victory before the throne on a sea of glass—the great antitype of "the table that is before the Lord" (Ezek. 41:22; see also Rev. 4:6; 14:1–5; 15:2).

As the sacred table of Ezekiel's temple stands before the open doors of the Holiest, presenting the twelve unleavened loaves, so the twelve tribes of Israel will be presented before God on Mount Zion without fault.

And I saw, and behold, the Lamb standing on the mount Zion, and with him a hundred and forty and four thousand, having his name, and the name of his Father, written on their foreheads. And I heard a voice from heaven, as the voice of many waters, and as the voice of a great thunder: and the voice which I heard was as the voice of harpers harping with their harps: and they sing as it were a new song before the throne, and before the four living creatures and the elders: and no man could learn the song save the hundred and forty and four thousand, even they that had been purchased out of the earth. These are they that were not defiled with women; for they are virgins. These are they that follow the Lamb whithersoever he goeth. These were purchased from among men, to be the firstfruits unto God and unto the Lamb. And in their mouth was found no lie: they are without blemish. (Revelation 14:1–5)

The 144,000

Earlier, we looked at this topic briefly, but let's revisit it here and ask the question again: Who are the 144,000? This group is not mentioned anywhere in the Bible except in Revelation. This suggests their identity is not revealed fully until the end times, but inspiration gives us a preview to enable us to correctly identify them when they do appear.

In Revelation 7, we're told they are composed of the 12 tribes of Israel, 12,000 per tribe, for a total of 144,000. In chapter 14, they are further identified as spiritual virgins, with no taint of sin or impurity on them. This is the best clue of who they are: They are the overcomers who obtain a decided victory over sin and follow the Lamb in all things, come what may.

They are also called the first fruits of Christ's atonement. They have a faith as great as or greater than the martyrs had. They follow the Lamb *wherever* He goes.

That may seem exceptional to us, but in heaven, that is the norm. The unfallen worlds and angels are all in complete harmony with the government of God and each other. They find their greatest joy in fulfilling His will. All created beings reflect the character of God, who's essence of being is unselfish love.

As noted previously, in the Levitical temple, we have a symbol of this group: The bread of the presence, twelve loaves, were placed on the table of showbread on the north side of the sanctuary. Mount Zion, where the tribes appear, is on the north side of the holy city.

Here is the description and arrangement of the showbread:

> And thou shalt take fine flour, and bake twelve cakes thereof: two tenth deals shall be in one cake. And thou shalt set them in two rows, six on a row, upon the pure table before the LORD. And thou shalt put pure frankincense upon *each* row, that it may be on the bread for a memorial,

even an offering made by fire unto the LORD. Every Sabbath he shall set it in order before the LORD continually, *being taken* from the children of Israel by an everlasting covenant. And it shall be Aaron's and his sons'; and they shall eat it in the holy place: for it *is* most holy unto him of the offerings of the LORD made by fire by a perpetual statute. (Leviticus 24:5–9)

Notice these loaves are "made by fire," well baked. Each Friday, at the beginning of the Sabbath, the old loaves were removed, and the frankincense that had garnished them was offered on the golden altar of incense. The loaves were replaced by fresh ones, and the old were eaten by the priests and their sons.

In the Levitical service, there is no direct prohibition against using leaven, a symbol of the ferment and corruption of sin, in the bread of the presence. In this service, the Most Holy Place is shut and God's glory is concealed, so it is possible they contained leaven. However, this isn't possible in Ezekiel's temple, where the table is directly before God, who is a consuming fire to sin.

In the Levitical service, the twelve loaves were initially set in order by Moses when the tabernacle was erected on the first day of the first month, one year after Israel left Egypt. This is also the first day of atonement in Ezekiel's atonement week.

Interestingly, Ezekiel's temple never discloses directly what is presented on this table. It implies its function is the same as that of the table of showbread in the tabernacle, but the silence suggests there are other offerings presented besides the twelve loaves.

In Revelation 7, where the twelve tribes are sealed and presented, there are also many other redeemed ones, a "great multitude that no man could number," who have "come out of great tribulation and have washed their robes and made them white in the blood of the Lamb" (verses 9, 14, ESV).

These are also presented before the throne of God. Like the Zadokite priesthood, which waits on God day and night, these also "serve him day and night in his temple" (verse 15).

In the Levitical model, Aaron and his sons were ordained during the first week of the first month when Moses erected the tabernacle, and from the second week forward, the sons of Aaron replaced the loaves at the commencement of the Sabbath (see Exod. 40:2, 22, 23; Num. 8, 9).

Significantly, in Ezekiel's model, the first feast after the spring atonement is the Passover week, also called the Feast of Unleavened Bread. And again in Ezekiel's model, the week-long fall feast is a second Passover, with identical offerings to those of the spring and an identical seven-day prohibition against leaven.

Therefore, what we have in Ezekiel's temple is apparently a complete prohibition of yeast or leaven, a symbol of sin, throughout not only the spring and fall feasts but also throughout the year within the sanctuary. This is consistent with the prohibition against the use of wine in the service, which is also fermented by yeast or leaven. It underlines the point that leaven, a symbol of sin, is not found within Ezekiel's temple at any time of the year.

At the last supper, Christ used the unleavened Passover bread to represent His body and unfermented wine to represent His blood. In the case of the wine, He took an oath, promising He would not taste it again until He drinks it with us in His kingdom. In Ezekiel's temple, the absence of wine is a reminder that our Prince is abstaining from it in anticipation of his long-awaited reunion with us. When He breaks His fast, He will rejoice over His bride with fresh, new wine at the marriage supper of the Lamb.

A final word before leaving this topic: Beware of those who teach the doctrine of sin and live—who claim the leaven of sin in humanity is a permanent condition and the intercession of Christ will never cease. The services of both temple arrangements and the record of Revelation show that the intercessory work of Christ will be effective in us, and once the atonement of the Prince is complete, it will come to an end.

The end-time saints will be settled and sealed in the truth, not only through the judicial work performed at the cross but also through the fulfillment of that wonderful new covenant promise that the law will be written on our hearts through the mediation of Christ.

Ezekiel's temple vision promises us that the table of the presence will be placed before the Holiest. And in Revelation, we're assured that the bride will be gifted her spotless linen gown. "It was granted her to clothe herself with fine linen, bright and pure"— for the fine linen is the righteous deeds of the saints" (19:8). A sight to behold, she "looks forth as the morning, fair as the moon, clear as the sun, terrible as an army with banners" (Song of Sol. 6:10).

God's love is broad and deep. He loves us individually *and* collectively. The church is His bride, and she actually ravishes His heart with one glance of her eyes (see 4:9). This is hard to fathom. God not only *is* love; He is *in* love … with us, His church, the least deserving group of all His creation yet the apple of His eye. Amazing love!

Chapter 22

The Golden Altar and the Investigative Judgment

In chapter 9, I reviewed the Levitical Day of Atonement and Ezekiel's week of atonement provisions from the perspective of their cleansing and purification of the heavenly sanctuary. In this chapter, we'll look at the same subject but from the perspective of measuring and judgment—in particular, from the perspective of what Adventists call the "investigative judgment" that takes place at the close of the 2,300 days: "And he said unto me, Unto two thousand and three hundred days; then shall the sanctuary be cleansed" (Dan. 8:14).

In the Levitical tabernacle, the Most Holy Place was separated from the Holy Place by a thick, colorful, beautifully embroidered linen veil. The Day of Atonement was the only day of the year when the high priest was permitted to lift the veil and enter the direct presence of God, and then only with blood and incense. At the cross, this veil of separation between the Holy and Most Holy places was torn asunder by the torn body and heart of Christ, who opened for us the "new and living way" (Heb. 10:20).

The Levitical Day of Atonement was prophetic of the removal of the veil by Christ. It also typified the final cleansing of the sanctuary foretold by Gabriel that would commence at the close of the 2,300 prophetic days.[26] We understand from Daniel 9:24–27 and history that the starting point of the 2,300 years was 457 BC, when King Artaxerxes issued the command

---

[26] That the 2,300 days stand for 2,300 literal years is seen in the interpretation Gabriel gave to Daniel (see ch. 9), which links the 70 weeks (i.e., 490 years) to this prophecy and marks their commencement.

to restore and build Jerusalem. Adding 2,300 years to that date brings us to 1844.[27]

Since that year, Christ has been conducting His final atonement, which includes an investigation of the books of record. There are two stages to this cleansing work: The cases of the dead are judged first by reviewing the records of their lives; and then the cases of the living are reviewed.

Regarding the living, the purpose of this examination is both intercessory and judicial; it is to both empower God's people to overcome and also determine who is an overcomer and worthy of eternal life. This is necessary because when Christ returns, He brings His reward of immortality with Him. To ensure those who are redeemed are worthy, the church on earth must be judged prior to His return—their cases investigated.

In the parable of the wedding supper, this is represented by the king inspecting the guests to ensure all of them have on the wedding garment he graciously supplied (see Matt. 22:2–14). In that parable, the king found that not everyone present had on the required dress. He approached a man who didn't and asked him, "Friend, how camest thou in hither not having a wedding garment?" (verse 12). The man was speechless.

This process of inspecting the wedding guests began with the cases of the dead in 1844 at the close of the 2,300 days. While we don't know in advance when the transition takes place from the cases of the dead to the living, there are key scriptures that enable us to determine where we stand prophetically. The symbolism of the ancient worship services performed at the altars is key to understanding this.

The focal point of worship in the Levitical service was the ministry of the priests at the bronze and golden altars, which are in a straight east-west line that terminates in the Most Holy Place, the throne room of God. The primary function of the bronze altar was the atonement of sin by applying the blood to its horns and sides and the consumption by fire of the fat and flesh. As noted earlier, to sin, God is a consuming fire (see Heb. 12:29).

In contrast to the atonement of the bronze altar, the function of the golden altar was continual intercession, represented by the offering of incense twice daily, morning and evening, throughout the year. Regarding the golden altar, God instructed Moses:

---

[27] Here's the math: 1844 = -457 + 2,300 + 1. The extra year has to be added to the end of the equation to account for the lack of a 0 year between the BC and AD eras.

You shall make an altar to burn incense on; you shall make it of acacia wood.... And you shall overlay ... with pure gold ... And you shall put it before the veil that *is* before the ark of the Testimony, before the mercy seat that *is* over the Testimony, where I will meet with you ["you" refers to Moses and the priests]. Aaron shall burn on it sweet incense every morning; when he tends the lamps, he shall burn incense on it.... And Aaron shall make atonement upon its horns once a year with the blood of the sin offering of atonement ... It *is* most holy to the Lord. (Exodus 30:1, 3, 6, 7, 10, NKJV)

Notice the blood atonement and cleansing at the golden altar was a once-a-year event. What does this prefigure?

In Revelation 6:9–10, when the fifth seal opened, John saw the souls of the saints who had been slain for the Word of God. Where did he see them? Under this altar of intercession. They cried to the Lord, asking how long it will be before He will judge and avenge them of their murderers. Notice carefully that God hears their cry *and* issues judgment in their favor, giving them white robes. These are the royal garments of the wedding supper that the martyrs receive from the king and all who are called to the supper must have.

> This granting of garments to the martyrs is an important milestone in the investigative judgment and the cleansing of the sanctuary. After receiving their robes, they are told to wait patiently a little longer until their number is completed with those who are to give their lives as a witness to their faith. This is the final phase of the investigative judgment of the dead, which occurs during a time of martyrdom for the sake of Christ. This is taking place in many parts of the world today.

This granting of garments to the martyrs is an important milestone in the investigative judgment and the cleansing of the sanctuary. After receiving their robes, they are told to wait patiently a little longer until their number is completed with those who are to give their lives as a witness to their faith. This is the final phase of the investigative judgment of the dead, which occurs during a time of martyrdom for the sake of Christ. This is taking place in many parts of the world today. Notice this is the *fifth* seal.

However, the atonement of the golden altar is still not complete. In Revelation 8:3, at the breaking of the *seventh* seal, an angel, symbolic of Christ, stands before the golden altar with "much incense" to mingle with the prayers of the human intercessors. For what are the saints so earnestly praying that it becomes expedient to mingle "much incense" with their prayers? A special endowment of the Holy Spirit? Deliverance from oppression and martyrdom?

No doubt, it's both. And just as God answers the petitions of the martyrs in the fifth seal, in the seventh, He answers the petitions of the living, praying saints. As their prayers rise before Him, Christ mingles them with the fragrant incense of His righteousness, which encircles the throne of God. In response to their petitions, the Father glorifies His Son, who is given holy fire from the golden altar to shower upon the earth, specifically upon His waiting saints.

As Isaiah's lips were anointed at his commissioning with a live coal from the golden altar, in the same way, the lips of God's people are cleansed with fire from this same altar to witness powerfully for the truth. Notice the parallels between Isaiah 6 and Revelation 8. In both cases, the results are the same: Unprecedented judgments immediately follow the anointing as the seven trumpets sound. In Isaiah's day, cities were "laid waste," and the land of the rebels became "utterly desolate" (6:11).

Isaiah is a type of the Elijah people who will stand for God at the end of time. Revelation 8 shows that those who are empowered with fire from the altar warn the inhabitants of the earth of God's impending judgments. The results of this empowerment are also described in chapters 10 and 11. We have inspired commentary on Revelation 10:

> The mighty angel who instructed John was no less a personage than Jesus Christ. Setting His right foot on the sea, and His left upon the dry land, shows the part which He is acting in the closing scenes of the great controversy with Satan. This position denotes His supreme power and authority over the whole earth. The controversy has waxed stronger and more determined from age to age, and will continue to do so, to the concluding scenes when the masterly working of the powers of darkness shall reach their height. Satan, united with evil men, will deceive the whole world and the churches who receive not the love of the truth. *But the mighty angel demands attention. He cries with a loud voice. He is to show the power and authority of His voice to those who have united with Satan to oppose the truth.* After these seven thunders uttered their voices, the injunction comes to John as to Daniel in regard to the little book: "Seal up those things which the seven thunders uttered" (Revelation 10:4). These relate to future events which

will be disclosed in their order. Daniel shall stand in his lot at the end of the days. John sees the little book unsealed. Then Daniel's prophecies have their proper place in the first, second, and third angels' messages to be given to the world. (White, *Manuscript Releases*, vol. 1, p. 99, emphasis added)

In the emphasized portion above, notice God will empower this angel to cry with a mighty voice so as to capture the earth's attention. How will human interest be arrested? Placing this prophecy in the context of end-time events, we know God's judgments on the earth will be one of the primary means.

The intervention of God is in response to those who have united with the wicked and Satan to "deceive the whole world and the churches who receive not the love of the truth." What religiopolitical power is it that attempts to pervert true religion at the end of human history?

Revelation tells us spiritual Babylon will attempt such a feat. In mercy God, sends warning judgments to awaken the nations to the fallen, corrupt condition of the harlot, Babylon the Great. Prophecy foretells, however, that neither the nations that fornicate with her nor Babylon herself will repent.

Chapter 23

The Judgment of the Living

The fifth chapter of Revelation needs to be closely studied. It is of great importance to those who shall act a part in the work of God for these last days. There are some who are deceived. They do not realize what is coming on the earth.... Unless they make a decided change they will be found wanting when God pronounces judgment upon the children of men. They have transgressed the law and broken the everlasting covenant, and they will receive according to their works.

Testimonies for the Church, *vol. 9, p. 267, emphasis added*

In the quote above, Ellen White links Revelation 5, when Christ takes the scroll in hand, with judgment day. Ezekiel and Peter tell us judgment starts at the sanctuary with the household of God (see Ezek. 8, 9; 1 Peter 4:17).

In the last chapter, I suggested the judgment of the dead is depicted in the fifth seal at the golden altar and the judgment of the living is depicted in the seventh seal at the same altar. This agrees with the sequence of the Day of Atonement in the Levitical service. The golden altar is the last item cleansed.

This is also consistent with the altar scene in Revelation 8. Unlike in the fifth seal, where the dead petition God for justice, here in the seventh, it's the living saints who implore God for deliverance. As they petition God, their prayers are mingled by the Angel with incense upon the golden altar and come up before God as a fragrant aroma.

God calls for this strong, persistent intercession, urging us to cry between the porch and the altar for Him to spare His people (see Joel 2:17). The Lord is now bending low to us, listening for the prayer of faith that will unlock the treasure of heaven. Every sincere prayer is heard. Not one goes unanswered.

How are the living judged? Primarily by 1) the trials God allows to befall them to show them their weak points and thus strengthen and nurture them; and 2) their reception or rejection of truth. These critical situations test the quality of their faith and measure their fidelity to the truth under pressure.

Unfortunately, many fail the test. Speaking of this, Christ said, "And this is the judgment, that light is come into the world, and men loved darkness rather than the light; for their works were evil" (John 3:19, ESV).

Notwithstanding, many others pass the test with flying colors. It is the tremendous heat and pressure of nature that produces diamonds, and in the end, there will be many of them: "And those who are wise shall shine like the brightness of the sky above; and those who turn many to righteousness, like the stars forever and ever" (Dan. 12:2).

It is critical now for us to monitor our spiritual health and, with the help of the Holy Spirit, take candid inventory of our walk. Does Christ have all of our hearts? Are we listening to God in all areas of life? Are we at peace, as far as possible, with our families, friends, *and* enemies? If so, then we can say the Lord's prayer from our hearts and know He hears us.

Let me ask this: According to the prophets, when will the world be flooded with the light of truth? Doesn't this occur at the latter rain?

The judgment of the living and the latter rain are therefore concurrent and inseparable. When the gospel of Christ arrests the attention of the world by the power of the Spirit, the world is convicted of sin, righteousness, and judgment. This is why the first angel's message combines the hour of judgment with the everlasting gospel. They go hand in hand.

With that said, who has had more light on the gospel, the plan of salvation, and the sacrifice of Christ than anyone else has? Protestants in general and Seventh-day Adventists in particular. Therefore, we are the first to be judged. God's people are accountable today for our stewardship of the light we have been given, and in the future, the world will also be called to account at the outpouring of the latter rain.

Let us examine some inspired commentary on Ezekiel 9:

> He who presides over His church and the destinies of nations is carrying forward the last work to be accomplished for this world. To His angels He gives the commission to execute His judgments. Let the ministers awake, let them take in the situation. The work of judgment begins at the sanctuary.

"And behold, six men came from the way of the higher gate, which lieth toward the north, and every man a slaughter weapon in his hand; and one man among them was clothed with linen, with a writer's inkhorn by his side: and they went in, and stood beside the brazen altar." Read Ezekiel 9:2–7. The command is, "Slay utterly old and young, both maids, and little children, and woman: but come not near any man upon whom is the mark; and begin at My sanctuary. Then they began at the ancient men which were before the house." Saith God. "I will recompense their way upon their head." (White, *Testimonies to Ministers and Gospel Workers*, pp. 431, 432)

The judgment of the living is not instantaneous. It is the process of responding to light, and that takes time. The initial part of that process is pictured in Ezekiel 8–11. This vision is the precursor to his temple vision. In chapters 8–11, Israel is judged and scattered, and the glory of God reluctantly departs, leaving the temple desolate (see 11:19–23), whereas in the restored temple, the glory of God permanently returns (see 43:7)!

However, notice the shaking of God's people occurs first. Laodicea, meaning "a people judged," is where judgment begins. As with apostate Israel, its candlestick is removed, and then the rejuvenated church, like the rejuvenated nation, appears, represented by the seven spirits and seven lamps of fire sent into all the earth:

And there were seven lamps of fire burning before the throne, which are the seven Spirits of God.... And I beheld, and, lo, in the midst of the throne and of the four beasts, and in the midst of the elders, stood a Lamb as it had been slain, having seven horns and seven eyes, which are the seven Spirits of God sent forth into all the earth. (Revelation 4:5, 5:6)

This remnant church, like Laodicea, is not perfect. If it was, there would not be any need for its atonement. Rather, it is in a condition that allows the glory of the Lord to return to complete the cleansing process and seal the saints permanently in the truth. The good news is that when the divine surgery is complete, the image of God and Christ is restored in His bride—permanently.

***

The Hebrew word for "atonement," *kaphar*, means "to cover" and connotes mercy, pardon, forgiveness, expiation, cleansing, and reconciliation.

The righteousness of Christ, illustrated in the parable of the wedding garment, is not a cover to conceal sin; it is a complete renovation of character by His mediation. This is a process requiring our undivided hearts and full cooperation. Christ provides the power and grants us His grace; we make the choices; these, He leaves to us.

> "The righteousness of Christ, illustrated in the parable of the wedding garment, is not a cover to conceal sin; it is a complete renovation of character by His mediation. This is a process requiring our undivided hearts and full cooperation. Christ provides the power and grants us His grace."

Chapter 24

The Offerings of the People

The offerings of the Hebrew sanctuary were, first and foremost, substitutionary in nature. The first fruits went for the whole product; the firstlings, for the flock; the redemption money, for the individual. In the case of the animal sacrifices, the principle of substitution reaches its paradigm. Here, the life of the animal, represented by its blood, is accepted in substitution for the life of the penitent.

Besides the corporate festival offerings, God instructed the people to bring their personal offerings, which He divided into four kinds: burnt offerings, grain offerings, peace offerings, and sin offerings. We will now look briefly at these.

Burnt Offerings

Regarding the individual burnt offering, like the corporate burnt offering, the penitent led his sacrifice to the altar, placed his hand on the head of the animal, confessed his sin, and then cut its throat with his own hands. The priest caught the stream of blood, which he sprinkled against all four sides of the bronze altar, and then the entire animal, except for its hide—that is, every living part—was, after being washed, offered on the altar. The offeror flayed and parted the animal, and the hide was given to the priest who had applied the blood (see Lev. 1:3–17; 7:8).

Like the corporate burnt offerings which were accompanied by corresponding grain offerings and wine libations, the same law applied to individual offerings (see Num. 15:1-16).

The whole burnt offering, a freewill offering, symbolized both the sacrifice of Christ, who gave all of Himself willingly for us, and the worshiper's response of gratitude and entire consecration to God.

Grain Offerings

The next individual offering on the Levitical list was the grain offering (see ch. 2—called the "meat offering" in the KJV). If the offering was fine flour, it was to be moistened with oil and accompanied by frankincense. If it was cooked or baked, frankincense was not required, but it was to be mixed with oil and baked without leaven, honey, or sweetener. In all cases, the grain offering was to be salted with the "salt of the covenant" (see verse 13).

The oil, of course, represents the intercession of the Holy Spirit, which makes our gifts acceptable to God. By the frankincense of Christ's righteousness, the Spirit lifts our souls out of sin into the pure atmosphere of heaven.

The salt of the covenant represents the believer's response of faith. No offering to God is possible or acceptable to Him without it. The believer's faith has no merit in itself, but it reaches out of itself and grasps the righteousness of Christ. This faith is not merely an intellectual ascent to the truth; it is the gift of Christ working in individuals, enabling them to place their wills completely on the side of righteousness. As the person encounters various tests and trials, a Christian "worth his [weight in] salt" acts in the strength of Christ regardless of feeling.

Christ said, "Ye are the salt of the earth" (Matt. 5:13). He commends those who, like the men and women of Hebrews 11 did, combine belief with action. These are the unsung heroes of earth who for generations have preserved the world by the salt of their holy influence.

The quantity of flour for the grain offering is unspecified. Like the whole burnt offering, it was a freewill offering and could be small or large. The Lord values each offering by the love and cheerfulness of the giver. The poor widow's two mites was of far more value to God than was all the gifts the wealthy gave from their excess.

Peace Offerings

The third individual offering on the Levitical list was the peace offering, also a freewill offering, which shared many similarities with the burnt offering, the main difference being that the flesh of the peace offering was shared by the priest, his sons, the offeror, and his family. The specifications, which are worth our study but can't be covered here, are found mainly in Leviticus 3 and 7:11–34.

Sin Offerings

The fourth kind of individual offerings were the various sin offerings (see 4:1–7:10). Books could be written on these, and if time permits, I may eventually update this book and offer some commentary. For now, I'll confine myself to a few prominent features of the sin offerings.

Notice first that sin offerings are fourth and last on the list of individual offerings. Ever since the fall of Adam, sin has been the cause of death, decay, and the curse of human nature, inclining it to evil. At first glance, it may seem odd that sin offerings are last on the list, but here, inspiration is helping us prioritize according to God's priorities.

In placing the burnt offering first, God is saying, first and foremost, He wants our undivided hearts. The whole, complete surrender of ourselves to God in gratitude for His goodness to us is the remedy for our sin and where we need to begin because this is where the new birth occurs. By His Spirit, He draws us, and in yielding ourselves fully to Him, the chains of self and sin are broken by a miracle of grace. We are God's whole burnt offerings.

The Lord's next priority is that we are unselfish in our service to others and Him; this is represented by the grain offerings, which are acts of gratitude, entirely of our free will. Then God places the peace offerings next to encourage us to be at peace, first with Him, then with ourselves, our families, and neighbors, as far as it's in our power.

When we have our priorities aligned with God's, then we're in a position where He can perform His delicate surgery, removing the remaining tumors of sin that disfigure us and fully restoring us to His image.

Regarding the particulars of the sin offerings, notice in Leviticus 4 how sin is expiated: by blood on the four horns of the altar hearth. In the case of the burnt and peace offerings, the blood was applied to the sides of the altar, never to its horns. However, for sin offerings, the opposite is true; blood is not applied to the sides but always to the four horns, and the remainder of the blood is poured out at the base of the altar. The excess blood does not cleanse the altar; it is discarded.[28]

---

[28] The only exception to this rule is in cases where the offeror cannot afford a lamb. In the place of the lamb, the poor can bring a pair of pigeons or doves, one for a sin offering and one for a burnt offering, and in this case, some of the blood of the sin offering is sprinkled on the sides of the altar. The reason for the change appears to be that the animal sacrifices are slain by cutting the main neck artery so the animal dies by the loss of its blood. According to Scripture, the life is in the blood. In contrast, in the case of the birds, the death is caused by removing the head, so the blood cannot be used on the four horns.

In Scripture (and many heathen religions), horns represent power. Inspiration tells us the sting of death is sin and the power of sin is the law (see 1 Cor. 15:56). The record of our sins that enslaves us in bondage to death is inscribed figuratively on the horns of the altar, a symbol of our consciences. These horns are what must be purged by the blood of Christ. When they are, the power of sin is broken. "The sin of Judah is written with a pen of iron, and with the point of a diamond: it is graven upon the table of their heart, and upon the horns of your altars" (Jer. 17:1).

Yes, sin is indeed powerful. It has an iron grip on the human heart, and no amount of animal blood, rituals, penance, good works, pilgrimages, fasts, dispensations, indulgences, or anything similar can cleanse it. However, the blood of Christ is all-powerful and can cleanse the deepest stains of our souls.

In an early vision (1849) given to Ellen White, called "The Sealing," she saw the following:

> I saw four angels who had a work to do on the earth, and were on their way to accomplish it. Jesus was clothed with priestly garments. He gazed in pity on the remnant, then raised His hands, and with a voice of deep pity cried, "*My blood, Father, My blood, My blood, My blood!*" Then I saw an exceeding bright light come from God, who sat upon the great white throne, and was shed all about Jesus. Then I saw an angel with a commission from Jesus, swiftly flying to the four angels who had a work to do on the earth, and waving something up and down in his hand, and crying with a loud voice, "*Hold! Hold! Hold! Hold!* until the servants of God are sealed in their foreheads." (White, *Early Writings*, p. 38)

Notice Jesus pleads His blood four times, the same number as the horns of the altar and the angels who were about to let go the winds of strife. As previously noted, in type, the last object cleansed on the Day of Atonement is the golden altar and its four horns (see Lev 16:18, 19; Rev. 9:13).

The sealing White recounted and the final cleansing of the golden altar in Leviticus and Revelation describe the same thing: the purging and sealing of the consciences of the end-time church. This process is well underway. We know that because in her vision and in Scripture, the four angels are being held back to give the sealing angel more time:

> And after these things I saw four angels standing on the four corners of the earth, holding the four winds of the earth, that the wind should

not blow on the earth, nor on the sea, nor on any tree. And I saw another angel ascending from the east, having the seal of the living God: and he cried with a loud voice to the four angels, to whom it was given to hurt the earth and the sea, Saying, *Hurt not the earth, neither the sea, nor the trees, till we have sealed the servants of our God in their foreheads....* And when he had opened the seventh seal, there was silence in heaven about the space of half an hour. And I saw the seven angels which stood before God; and to them were given seven trumpets. *And another angel came and stood at the altar, having a golden censer; and there was given unto him much incense, that he should offer it with the prayers of all saints upon the golden altar which was before the throne. And the smoke of the incense, which came with the prayers of the saints, ascended up before God out of the angel's hand.* And the angel took the censer, and filled it with fire of the altar, and cast it into the earth: and there were voices, and thunderings, and lightnings, and an earthquake. And the seven angels which had the seven trumpets prepared themselves to sound. The first angel sounded ... And the second angel sounded ... And the third angel sounded ... And the fourth angel sounded ... And the fifth angel sounded ... *And the sixth angel sounded, and I heard a voice from the four horns of the golden altar which is before God, Saying to the sixth angel which had the trumpet, Loose the four angels which are bound in the great river Euphrates.* And the four angels were loosed, which were prepared for an hour, and a day, and a month, and a year, for to slay the third part of men. (Revelation 7:1–3; 8:1–8, 10, 12; 9:1, 13–15, emphasis added)

Notice the progression in the emphasized portions. The four angels are held back from letting go of the winds of strife while Christ is pleading His blood, which is applied to the consciences of His people, sealing them in His character. This is the fulfilment of the new covenant—the blotting-out process Peter said would accompany the times of refreshing, the latter rain of the Holy Spirit.

In response to the intercession of Christ and the saints, fire is taken from the golden altar and scattered on the earth, followed by the trumpets sounding one after another in rapid succession (see 8:1–5).

With that said, notice, during the trumpets, the four angels are not

> The four angels are held back from letting go of the winds of strife while Christ is pleading His blood, which is applied to the consciences of His people, sealing them in His character. This is the fulfilment of the new covenant.

fully released until the horns of the golden altar, a symbol of the living church, is purged. When the sixth trumpet sounds, a voice issues from its horns, indicating its cleansing is complete. Then the winds of strife are fully released (see 9:13).

The full release of the winds marks the close of probation. Those who remain alive on the earth who are not sealed by the end of this trumpet are beyond repentance. Scripture says they do not repent:

> And the rest of the men which were not killed by these plagues yet repented not of the works of their hands, that they should not worship devils, and idols of gold, and silver, and brass, and stone, and of wood: which neither can see, nor hear, nor walk: Neither repented they of their murders, nor of their sorceries, nor of their fornication, nor of their thefts. (Revelation 9:20, 21)

Chapter 25

The Corporate Offerings

During the feasts of the Levitical service, in addition to the daily burnt offering, there were corporate burnt offerings that varied with each feast. As noted earlier, the Levitical corporate offerings were markedly different from those in Ezekiel's temple. With the former, the prescribed burnt offering for the spring convocations, the feasts of Passover and Firstfruits, was two bulls,[29] one ram and seven lambs together with the prescribed grain offerings and wine libations. This was offered on each day of the feasts together with a male goat for a sin offering—the sin offering always following the burnt offering.

However, in Ezekiel's temple, the prescribed burnt offering has changed. Regarding the Passover burnt offering, rather than two bulls, one ram, and seven lambs as offered in the Levitical service, in Ezekiel's service, the corporate burnt offering is much richer in both animals and accompanying flour oblations: seven bulls and seven rams with an ephah of fine flour per animal mixed with an equally generous amount of oil.

Why the change? One clue is the type of animals. In Ezekiel's temple, no young lambs are offered—the offering of the common people—but instead, bulls are offered; they were the offering of a priest. Additionally, rather than two bulls, as in the Levitical system, there are seven, indicating the nation has become a nation of priests. Furthermore, rather than one ram, the offering of a ruler, there are seven, indicating the nation has become a nation of priest-kings.

---

[29] There is a difference between the number of bulls and rams included in the burnt offering of the Feast of Firstfruits in Numbers 28:27 compared to Leviticus 23:18. The reason for the difference is that the burnt offering in Leviticus accompanies the public peace offering of the two lambs and two loaves of the first fruits that are waved, while the burnt offering in Numbers is the festal burnt offering for the feast itself.

This is confirmed in the grain offerings that accompany the animals: In the Levitical model, the grain offering with the ram was less than that with the bull, whereas in Ezekiel's temple, it is identical, meaning the offering is for the same royal priesthood, the line of Melchizedek, which combines the offices of both priests and kings in the same persons.

Balaam's Prophecy

Another clue to the meaning of the sevenfold offerings of Ezekiel's temple is the burnt offering of King Balak of Moab, who hired Balaam to curse Israel just before they took possession of the Promised Land. When Balaam attempted to curse Israel three times that day, each time, he started with this offering, seven bulls and seven rams, and instead of cursing them, he blessed them. At the end of the day, after the final attempt, Balaam prophesied:

> I shall see him, but not now: I shall behold him, but not nigh: there shall come a Star out of Jacob, and a Sceptre shall rise out of Israel, and shall smite the corners of Moab, and destroy all the children of Sheth. And Edom shall be a possession, Seir also shall be a possession for his enemies; and Israel shall do valiantly. Out of Jacob shall come he that shall have dominion, and shall destroy him that remaineth of the city.... Alas, who shall live when God doeth this! And ships *shall come* from the coast of Chittim, and shall afflict Asshur, and shall afflict Eber, and he also shall perish for ever. (Numbers 24:17–19; 23, 24)

This prophecy has a dual application: first, to Israel's conquest of Canaan; and second, to spiritual Israel at the end, when the little horn power attempts to curse Israel again, but a Star and a Scepter of David arises: the Prince of the covenant. The seven bulls and seven rams of Balaam's offering points us forward to the royal priesthood of Ezekiel's temple, the seven eyes and seven fiery lamps of the Lamb, and the complete, sevenfold atonement of the new covenant and the eternal kingdom of our Prince (see Dan 2, 7–12; Rev. 4, 5).

Hezekiah Cleanses the Temple

Interestingly, the same burnt offering, seven bulls and seven rams, was also used by King Hezekiah seven centuries later, when he cleansed the temple and renewed Judah's covenant with God after the sixteen-year reign of his idolatrous father, King Ahaz, who had closed the temple doors:

> Hezekiah began to reign when he was twenty-five years old ... And he did what was right in the eyes of the LORD, according to all that David his father had done. In the first year of his reign, in the first month, he opened the doors of the house of the LORD and repaired them. He brought in the priests and the Levites and assembled them in the square on the east and said to them, "Hear me, Levites! Now consecrate yourselves, and consecrate the house of the LORD, the God of your fathers, and carry out the filth from the Holy Place. For our fathers have been unfaithful and have done what was evil in the sight of the LORD our God. They have forsaken him and have turned away their faces from the habitation of the LORD and turned their backs (2 Chron. 29:1–6).

The Levites responded to the king's exhortation with zeal and promptly set to work to cleanse and restore the sanctuary.

> Then the Levites arose ... gathered their brothers and consecrated themselves and went in as the king had commanded, by the words of the LORD, to cleanse the house of the LORD ... *They began to consecrate on the first day of the first month, and on the eighth day of the month they came to the vestibule of the LORD. Then for eight days they consecrated the house of the LORD, and on the sixteenth day of the first month they finished.* Then they went in to Hezekiah the king and said, "We have cleansed all the house of the LORD, the altar of burnt offering and all its utensils, and the table for the showbread and all its utensils. All the utensils that King Ahaz discarded in his reign when he was faithless, we have made ready and consecrated, and behold, they are before the altar of the LORD." Then Hezekiah the king rose early and gathered the officials of the city and went up to the house of the LORD. *And they brought seven bulls, seven rams, seven lambs [for a burnt offering], and seven male goats for a sin offering for the kingdom and for the sanctuary and for Judah.* And he commanded the priests, the sons of Aaron, to offer them on the altar of the LORD ... And Hezekiah and all the people rejoiced because God had provided for the people, for the thing came about suddenly (2 Chronicles 29:12, 15, 17, 20, 21, 36, emphasis added).

Hezekiah, like Melchizedek, was a type of the Prince of the covenant of Ezekiel's temple. Let's look briefly at some of the parallels:

1. The priests under Hezekiah cleansed the first temple (Solomon's) starting on the first day of the year for seven days, just as there is a seven-day atonement at the start of the year in Ezekiel's temple (see 2 Chron. 29:16–18; Ezek. 45:18–20).
2. The cleansing of the temple by Hezekiah was completed on the sixteenth day of the first month, the Feast of Firstfruits, a symbol of the 144,000. In keeping with Firstfruits and Ezekiel's model, rather than offering the Levitical burnt offering (two bulls, one ram, and seven lambs), Hezekiah instead offered seven bulls and seven rams, as in the Passover ritual of Ezekiel's temple, given in vision over 100 years later (see 2 Chron. 29:21–23; Ezek. 45:23).
3. Once the temple was cleansed, Hezekiah, as a type of the Prince of the covenant, renewed the covenant between God and Israel.

The covenant renewal by King Hezekiah contains the essence of Ezekiel's allegory: Hezekiah was a type of the Prince of the covenant who reigns on Mount Zion over God's people. "Glorious things are spoken of thee, O city of God" (Ps. 87:3).

The Goat Sin Offerings

One of the provisions of the feasts of both models is the requirement of the goat sin offering following the burnt offerings. On each of the thirty Levitical feast days (seven at Passover/Unleavened Bread/Firstfruits, one at Pentecost, one at Trumpets, one at the Day of Atonement, eight at Tabernacles, and twelve new moons), a goat for a corporate sin offering followed and accompanied the burnt offering. In Ezekiel's temple, there are twenty-eight feast days (two days at the spring week of atonement, seven at Passover one week later, seven in the fall, and the twelve new moons), and like in the Levitical service, these are also followed by a goat sin offering, except—and these are important exceptions—1) for the week of atonement because on both days, first and seventh, the atonement ends with the offering of the bulls; and 2) for the new moon burnt offerings, which also have no sin offerings.

In the case of the week of atonement, when these two bulls are offered on the first and seventh days, there is no burnt offering or accompanying sin offering. This implies the atonement of the bull itself is the complete, final offering for Israel. And that agrees with the burnt offerings of the new moons. They also have no sin offerings because they are no longer necessary.

The First Fruits Replacement

Under Levitical law, there were two annual first fruit offerings: 1) the offering of the first barley sheaf on the morning after the first Sabbath of Passover week, Nisan 16 (see Lev 23:7, 10, 11); and 2) the offering of the two loaves of first fruits fifty days later at Pentecost (see verses 15–21).

At the resurrection of Christ on the Feast of Firstfruits, many of the sleeping saints rose with Him as the first fruits of the wave sheaf. These ascended to heaven with Him fifty days later. In the type, fifty days after the barley sheaf was waved before the Lord, the two loaves of the first fruits were also waved. These two loaves represent two groups, in my opinion: 1) the saints who were raised with Christ and returned with Him to heaven; and 2) the believers who were added to the church at Pentecost, the first fruits of the gospel dispensation.

In Ezekiel's temple, the two loaves have been replaced by the *twelve* loaves of the bread of the presence, a permanent offering placed directly before the mercy seat.

> Today, we are on the threshold of something momentous: the time when Revelation's prophecies regarding the first fruits, the twelve tribes, will be presented to the Father by Christ. Just as the coronation of Christ at Pentecost was celebrated by the offering of the first fruits and the dispensation of the early rain, in the same way, at this greater, final glorification of Christ, when the Lion of the tribe of Judah takes the scroll, a still greater endowment of the Holy Spirit will be sent, empowering the church for the final gospel harvest.

Today, we are on the threshold of something momentous: the time when Revelation's prophecies regarding the first fruits, the twelve tribes of Revelation 7 and 14, will be presented to the Father by Christ. Just as the coronation of Christ at Pentecost was celebrated by the offering of the first fruits and the dispensation of the early rain (see Ps. 68:18; Eph. 4:8), in the same way, at this greater, final glorification of Christ, when the Lion of the tribe of Judah takes the scroll, a still greater endowment of the Holy Spirit will be sent, empowering the church for the final gospel harvest.

Chapter 26

The Seven-Day Cleansings

The week of atonement in Ezekiel's temple is far from unique in the ceremonial law. It is actually the norm, and the Levitical Day of Atonement is the exception. Under Levitical law, the cleansing service for individuals who became ceremonially unclean usually spanned seven days.[30] And the ordination services in both temples also span seven days. We'll look at four examples of cleansing and ordination in Leviticus below. The point of reviewing these is to shed light on the seven-day atonement of Ezekiel's temple, which parallels all four and helps us bring the practical application home.

The Red Heifer and the Dead

Under Mosaic law, besides the seven-day ordination service of the priesthood, there were four other seven-day purification rites that applied to the common Israelite: a woman after childbirth, those who had contact with the dead, a Nazarite who had contact with the dead, and a leper after being cured.

Regarding contact with the dead, a seven-day purification rite was enjoined on all Israelites: priest, Levite, commoner. The rite was simple yet beautiful in its simplicity (see Num. 19:11ff). The individual who had contact with a dead body was sprinkled with water mixed with the ashes

---

[30] In the case of a woman after childbirth, the woman was unclean for seven days for a male child, fourteen days for a female, and separated from the holy things of the sanctuary for another thirty-three and sixty-six days, respectively (see Lev. 12:1–7).

of a red heifer using a sprig of hyssop. The sprinkling was done on the third and seventh days after the defiling contact.

If the person could not be cleansed at that time, he or she remained unclean until that person could be. Because those who were ceremonially unclean were excluded from Israel's three annual feasts (Unleavened Bread, Pentecost, Tabernacles), it was necessary for any who were defiled to be cleansed before the next feast so they could participate in it.

The red heifer sacrifice that provided the ashes for cleansing was unique in a number of ways. First, its color was symbolic. In the law, the color of the sacrifice was never specified except in this case. Second, it was slain outside not only the temple but even the city, in a clean place, and this was where the ashes of the heifer were kept.

There was a clear connection with the sanctuary service, however, in that the heifer's blood was sprinkled seven times in the direction of the temple.

Third, this sacrifice defiled the offeror, making him ceremonially unclean. The high priest was not permitted to offer it due to the law, which required the high priest to remain ceremonially clean at all times (see Lev. 21:1–4). The offering of the heifer, therefore, was delegated to one of his subordinates.

The heifer shared similarities with the scapegoat of the Day of Atonement. Like with the scapegoat, anyone who touched the heifer after it became a sin offering was also unclean. In the case of the heifer, this fact is amplified by the rule that anyone who touched its ashes, the very ashes used to purify, also became unclean. And even the person who performed the sprinkling was required to wash his clothes afterward, although none of the cleansing water-and-ash mixture had touched him. If the mixture had touched him, he became unclean for seven days.

Like contact with the dead, any contact with the heifer or its ashes contaminated. And yet through the divine plan, the plague of contaminating evil was purged. Through the heifer's ashes, representing the sacrificial death of Christ, who suffered for us as a criminal outside the city, the punishment for Israel's defilement fell on the innocent animal. The blood sprinkled in the direction of the sanctuary represents the blood of Christ our sacrifice that sprinkles and cleanses us.

> So shall he sprinkle many nations; the kings shall shut their mouths at him: for that which had not been told them shall they see; and that which they had not heard shall they consider. (Isaiah 52:15)

The Unsolved Murder Heifer

Let's take a short detour from the seven-day cleansing rituals and now look briefly at another example of a heifer sacrifice—the murder heifer:

> If *one* be found slain in the land which the LORD thy God giveth thee to possess it, lying in the field, *and* it be not known who hath slain him: Then thy elders and thy judges shall come forth, and they shall measure unto the cities which *are* round about him that is slain: And it shall be, *that* the city *which is* next unto the slain man, even the elders of that city shall take an heifer, which hath not been wrought with, *and* which hath not drawn in the yoke; And the elders of that city shall bring down the heifer unto a rough valley, which is neither eared nor sown, and shall strike off the heifer's neck there in the valley: And the priests the sons of Levi shall come near; for them the LORD thy God hath chosen to minister unto him, and to bless in the name of the LORD; and by their word shall every controversy and every stroke be *tried:* And all the elders of that city, *that are* next unto the slain *man*, shall wash their hands over the heifer that is beheaded in the valley: And they shall answer and say, Our hands have not shed this blood, neither have our eyes seen *it.* Be merciful, O LORD, unto thy people Israel, whom thou hast redeemed, and lay not innocent blood unto thy people of Israel's charge. And the blood shall be forgiven them. So shalt thou put away the *guilt of* innocent blood from among you, when thou shalt do *that which is* right in the sight of the LORD. (Deuteronomy 21:1–9)

The similarities between the red heifer and the murder heifer above are many. In both cases, it was to be a young animal that had never been yoked, representing Christ, who, under no obligation, freely offered Himself in our place.

However, in the case of the murder heifer, there is not even a gesture towards the sanctuary, showing that while the guilt of the murderer in no way tainted the sanctuary, the innocent animal, representing Christ, still bore the penalty. This heifer was slain in a desolate, uninhabited valley. Christ was also the murder heifer, dying alone, forsaken by humanity and apparently His Father, who, in fact, suffered equally, if not more, with His Son.

The Cleansing of the Leper

Returning now to the seven-day cleansings, the ritual of the cleansed leper is especially interesting because, like in the spring atonement of Ezekiel's temple, a double cleansing occurs on the first and seventh days of this seven-day ritual as well. And there is a marked parallel with the Levitical Day of Atonement.

The process began outside the temple and city with a thorough inspection by the priest of the one who claimed to have been cured.[31] After the priest carefully examined the leper and found no taint of the disease, two clean birds were brought. The first bird was torn, and its blood was caught in a clay pot containing about twelve ounces (750 milliliters) of fresh-flowing ("living") water. The second bird was then dipped alive in the blood-and-water mixture along with cedar wood, hyssop, and scarlet wool. After sprinkling the man with the blood-water mixture seven times using the above three articles, the captive live bird, a symbol of the cleansed man, was released into the open field. The man then washed his clothes, shaved off all his hair, and bathed himself; then he was pronounced clean and permitted to reenter Israelite society.

Significantly, though, he was not permitted to resume his responsibilities as the head of his house or even enter his home until a second rite of purification was completed. This phase commenced after the man shaved and bathed. From that time, he was to wait outside his home for seven days and then, on the seventh day, wash his clothes, shave and bathe again, and present himself at the temple, bringing with him three animals: two male lambs, one as a sin offering and one as a burnt offering, and a ram for a fellowship offering.

The Scriptures clearly indicate the initial offering of two birds had cleansed the leper. The second set of offerings at the end of the seven-day period therefore has a higher purpose. This is evident in that the second service is a type of ordination similar in many respects to the ordination of the Aaronic priesthood, with the effect of restoring the man to the priesthood of his own house. Momentarily, we'll compare the two services in Leviticus 8–9 and 14.

---

[31] The Hebrew term for leprosy encompasses additional skin diseases.

Ordination and Atonement Services

I noted earlier that the ordination of the priesthood in the Levitical model took place during the first week of the first month, the same week as the atonement of Ezekiel's temple.

The Mosaic law generally required that the blood of the bull sin offering should be brought within the temple and applied to the four horns of the golden altar of incense (see Lev. 4:1–7). However, in the Levitical ordination service, the blood of the bull sin offering is applied only to the horns of the *bronze* altar, and it is specifically stated that its purpose is to sanctify the altar. In addition to the connection between the golden altar and the priesthood, a close relationship therefore also exists between the ordination of the priesthood and the sanctification of the bronze altar.

Significantly, in the Levitical service, a dedication service for the altar by the twelve tribes accompanied its sanctification during the priestly ordination. Its dedication by the tribes began on the same day, the first day of the first month, and spanned the following twelve days, one day for each tribe. Here is the summary of the total offerings that were offered over the course of the twelve days of dedication:

> All the oxen for the burnt offering were twelve bullocks, the rams twelve, the lambs of the first year twelve, with their meat offering: and the kids of the goats for sin offering twelve. And all the oxen for the sacrifice of the peace offerings were twenty and four bullocks, the rams sixty, the he goats sixty, the lambs of the first year sixty. This was the dedication of the altar, after that it was anointed. (Numbers 7:87, 88)

In Ezekiel's model, when the spring cleansing service (after the dedication service of the bronze altar) commences on the first day of the first month, the house of Zadok officiates (see Ezek. 45:18ff). This is in contrast to the Levitical model, where the Aaronic priesthood commences their priestly work only after their ordination on the eighth day (see Lev. 8, 9). The lesson for us here is that when Ezekiel's model is put in place, the priesthood of Zadok and the bronze altar will both have been previously sanctified and ordained.

Returning now to the consecration of both the cleansed leper and the Aaronic priesthood: In the case of the cured leper, a symbol of the cleansed sinner (recall he was already cleansed by the two birds and associated rites), the blood of a male lamb as a sin offering was first placed on the leper's right ear, right thumb, and right big toe. Next, the sacred oil, a symbol of the Holy Spirit, was then applied by the priest to the same three areas.

In the case of the Aaronic priesthood, the blood of a ram was applied to the same areas, and this was also followed by application of the holy oil, again to the right ear, right thumb, and right big toe. In both cases, the essential ingredients for ordination are the blood of the atonement and the oil of the Spirit. It is the blood of Christ and the oil of His Spirit that consecrates the sons and daughters of God for ministry.

Nevertheless, notice the ordination of the high priest differed from that of the subordinate priesthood in this way: Aaron's head and beard were anointed concurrently with the anointing of the tabernacle and the altar by Moses. This special anointing occurred *prior* to any of the blood sacrifices being offered, pointing us to the undefiled priesthood of Christ: "Thou lovest righteousness, and hatest wickedness: therefore God, thy God, hath anointed thee with the oil of gladness above thy fellows" (Ps. 45:7).

The Nazarite Vow

A Nazarite was an Israelite—priest, ruler, or commoner—who, under Mosaic law, made a voluntary vow of separation to the Lord. The vow could be for any length of time; it could even be for life. The three essentials of the Nazarite vow were total abstinence from wine, no ceremonial defilement by contact with the dead (even one's parents), and a prohibition against cutting or trimming hair growth (see Num. 6:2–6).

The separation began at the time the vow was uttered, and nothing was required to establish the vow other than the words that were spoken. Upon completion of the vow, the Nazarite was to attend the temple with a male lamb for a burnt offering, a female lamb for a sin offering, and a ram for a fellowship offering, along with the prescribed baked cereal offerings and wine libations (see verses 13–21).

One notable aspect of the release ceremony is in regard to the hair. As noted above, the hair was not to be trimmed for the duration of the vow, but on the vow's completion, after the sacrifice of the sin and burnt offerings, as the meat of the fellowship ram was being boiled for the ceremonial meal, all of the Nazarite's hair was shaved off and thrown into the fire that cooked the ram. Notice this is not the fire of the bronze altar but rather a non-sacred cooking fire similar to the one that burned the red heifer outside the city. The significance of the shorn hair itself (as opposed to the fire) relates to the Holy Spirit.

The glory of a woman is said in the New Testament to be her long, beautiful hair (see 1 Cor. 11:15). The outward sign of the Nazarite's submission or separation to God was his hair. Samson was a Nazarite. His incredible strength was symbolic of the moral strength of the individual who is in subjection to the will of God. He is spiritually invincible. Whoever is born of God *cannot* sin (see 1 John 3:9). When Samson's hair was cut, the outward sign of his submission to God was removed, and his strength was removed with it.

In the sanctuary, the holy anointing oil, a symbol of the Holy Spirit, was placed on the hair of Aaron and his sons—on their heads and beards. Like with Samson, when the hair of the Nazarite is cut and shaved at the end of his vow, it showed in symbol that the one who is no longer in subjection or separation to Christ is devoid of the Spirit and therefore weak and powerless to resist evil.

Purification of the Nazarite

The ceremonial defilement of the Nazarite by the dead necessitated a cleansing just as in the case of contact with the dead by any common Israelite. However, the service to purify the Nazarite was a much more rigorous procedure. Whereas common Israelites were simply sprinkled with water mixed with the heifer's ashes on the third and seventh days of their cleansing, Nazarites, like lepers, were required to shave off their hair on the first day of their cleansing and again shave their hair on the seventh day. And, like lepers, on the seventh day, they were to bring two birds, one for a sin offering and one for a burnt offering, as well as a lamb for a guilt offering. And then their vow could be reinstated, but with the provision that none of the time they had been under vow prior to defilement counted!

This last provision may seem extreme, but clearly, the spiritual lessons here are the nub of the matter. And the Nazarite vow is a significant illustration, but of what? Of the process of sanctification. The Nazarite is a symbol of the person who has vowed to give his heart and life to God. From the time the vow is made, a living relationship with God and Christ exists.

Nevertheless, contact with sin, even unintentional, brings spiritual defilement. And any defilement has its consequences, even the unintentional. The punishment of Moses on the boarders of the Promised Land is a pointed reminder of this. All of Moses' long, exemplary service to

God and Israel could not undo his transgression or its consequences, even though his failure was unintentional.

Moses, caught off his guard, failed to critically examine his personal feelings before acting and unwittingly mistook his passions for righteous indignation. As a result, he knowingly disobeyed the command of God to speak to the rock and instead struck it twice. Yet even here, God overruled, and after Moses was denied his fondest dream, crossing the Jordan, he was resurrected by Christ and royally welcomed into a better land (see Jude 9).

Interestingly, under Ezekiel's model, no serving priest could be a Nazarite. This is not stated directly, but it is inferred because the Zadokite order were prohibited from shaving their heads or allowing their hair to grow long (Ezek. 44:20). The reason for this is the Zadokite priesthood had already been separated.

Like the Nazarites, the Zadokite priesthood was to abstain from wine (Ezek. 44:21). And similar to the Nazarites, they were not to defile themselves with the dead except in the case of a close relative, and in that case, like the Nazarites, they were not to minister until seven days after being purified, and on the seventh day, they were to offer a sin offering; then they would be accepted.

In the case of contact with the dead by the sons of Zadok, this is what was required:

> And they shall come at no dead person to defile themselves: but for father, or for mother, or for son, or for daughter, for brother, or for sister that hath had no husband, they may defile themselves. And after he is cleansed, they shall reckon unto him seven days. And in the day that he goeth into the sanctuary, unto the inner court, to minister in the sanctuary, he shall offer his sin offering, saith the Lord GOD. (Ezekiel 44:25–27)

Chapter 27

The Oath of Our Prince

The Waco Tragedy

One of the worst public relations disasters to befall the Adventist Church in the last century was the 1993 Waco massacre of Branch Davidians, an extreme offshoot of Seventh-day Adventism. On April 19 of that year, after a fifty-one-day siege, the FBI, the military, and Texas law enforcement launched an assault on the compound using incendiary tear gas bombs that caused it to go up in flames.[32] The world watched in horror as men, pregnant women, and many children burned to death. Seventy-eight members of the Davidians died.

> *Koresh had taken the Davidic restoration prophecies and applied them to himself as the branch of David. He skillfully used Scripture to bolster his claims and justify his debauchery.*

David Koresh, the cult leader, was one of the casualties. Koresh had taken the Davidic restoration prophecies and applied them to himself as the branch of David. He skillfully used Scripture to bolster his claims and justify his debauchery.

In all deceptions, there is an element of truth. The Scriptures, as we've seen, do in fact foretell the reestablishment of the throne of David in the

---

[32] It is still debated whether this action was the main cause of the inferno or if the Davidians assisted in burning the compound over themselves. It seems unlikely that pregnant women and their husbands would do that. This is evidence, in the author's opinion, that the mainstream media in 1993 was already well down the path of "fact checking" rather than providing unbiased journalism.

end times, not to a cult leader, but to the Son of David, who, at the end, stands up as our Prince and delivers His people.

The COVID Pandemic

Fast-forward now to 2024. During the last few years under the pandemic we've seen an unprecedented grab for power and a corresponding loss of liberty. This has been a window for the church on what lies ahead. Many innocent, loyal citizens were verbally attacked and socially ostracized. Many suffered the loss of jobs, careers, and businesses, were rejected by family, and made homeless for refusing the vaccine.

Even today, with the overwhelming evidence that these particular vaccines are neither safe nor effective,[33] the mainstream media and much of the health system is still in denial. Even now, after the "anti-vaxxers" (who, for the most part, were never opposed to properly tested conventional vaccines) have been vindicated, few journalists, leaders, or health professionals have apologized.

In the Adventist Church, most members in the West (North America, Europe, Australia, and New Zealand) continue to go blindly along with leaders who still don't see the mandates as an issue of conscience or liberty. This blindness is a terminal condition if it goes uncorrected because the renovation and restoration of the individual conscience is *the* essential work of Christ, the Mediator and Prince of the Covenant:

> For if the blood of bulls and of goats, and the ashes of an heifer sprinkling the unclean, sanctifieth to the purifying of the flesh: How much more shall the blood of Christ, who through the eternal Spirit offered himself without spot to God, purge your conscience from dead works to serve the living God? (Hebrews 9:13, 14)

Even if it could be shown that the safety concerns of the vaccines are completely unfounded, the issue of forcing the conscience would still remain. The Scriptures say our bodies are the temples of the Holy Spirit, and this fact makes the stewardship of our health a personal responsibility.

For more than a century, Adventists have understood that the main religious liberty issue at the end will be over the day of worship, Sabbath vs. Sunday, and the beast power will attempt to coerce the consciences of every person on that point. Because the issue of Sabbath sacredness was

---

[33] See https://1ref.us/mset1 and https://1ref.us/mset2.

not under debate during the pandemic, the majority of Western Adventists generally excused their silence and complicity, denying its relevance to the final battle of conscience between true and false worship.

Actually, the connection is strong and direct. In honoring the Sabbath, we honor the Creator, and in honoring our bodies as the temple of God, we honor the same Creator. Human institutions cross the line when they violate the bodily integrity of the individual, especially when they alter the building blocks of life and rewrite the life codes written by God Himself. Both the day of worship and the sanctity of human life relate directly back to the Author of life and our worship of Him.

The public has been erroneously taught that institutions of science and higher learning have an unrestricted right to improve the created order. While they do have a mandate to extend our knowledge of it, they have no mandate to play God by altering the life codes He has written. If they persist, they may find out too late that there are consequences; they do not know enough about the secrets of life of even the simplest organisms, such as viruses, to safely alter them. The escape of the coronavirus was a lesson that was lost on most.

Ellen White related a dream in which Christ addressed two particular Adventist Church leaders who held office in Battle Creek, Michigan, the headquarters of the church at that time (1874). In the dream, Christ said to them:

> Neither of you have seen the necessity of health reform, but when the plagues of God shall be all around you, you will then see the principles of health reform and strict temperance in all things,—that temperance alone is the foundation of all the graces that come from God, the foundation of all victories to be gained. (White, *Temperance*, p. 201)

Notice the warning Christ gives of more plagues to follow. Also notice the direct connection He makes between health reform, temperance, and safety during the plagues. Those who finally overcome and are sheltered during the plagues will be temperate in every aspect of their lives. Rejecting genetically modified vaccines is a part of temperance and health reform, which is a God-given responsibility.

Notwithstanding, let's bear in mind that God meets us where we are. When the pandemic began, most people believed the misinformation they were fed regarding the risks and effectiveness of the vaccines. They did what they thought was the right, responsible thing to do. God fully understands this and accepts their motives.

The Double Oath

The COVID pandemic was a harbinger of what lies ahead under the rule of the beast. However, the message from Ezekiel's temple vision to the ancient Jews and us today is that help is on the way—it's here even now. The Prince of the covenant, Christ, has accompanied us at every step of our journey so far, including through the pandemic. He has marked the sacrifices of His people for the sake of conscience and truth and is standing up on their behalf now as He always has.

This is a covenant relationship. For Christ to stand for us, we have to also stand for Him. The ordeal of the final refining fire, the mark of the beast, the Battle of Armageddon,[34] will test each saint closely, but Christ promises to stand with us in the fire like He did with the three Hebrews who would not bow down to and worship the image of the Babylonian king. To help us through what lies ahead, we find this unique promise Christ makes to us under oath:

> And the angel which I saw stand upon the sea and upon the earth lifted up his hand to heaven, *And sware by him that liveth for ever and ever … that there should be time no longer: But in the days of the voice of the seventh angel, when he shall begin to sound, the mystery of God should be finished, as he hath declared to his servants the prophets.* (Revelation 10:5–7, emphasis added)

We know the above oath is important because 1) Christ Himself makes it; He is the mighty angel; and 2) He swears by none other than God. Christ rarely makes such a solemn oath in Scripture, but in this case, He underlines its importance by making it twice. This is the other occurrence:

> And one said to the man clothed in linen, which was upon the waters of the river, How long shall it be to the end of these wonders? And I heard the man clothed in linen, which was upon the waters of the river, *when he held up his right hand and his left hand unto heaven, and sware by him that liveth for ever that it shall be for a time, times, and an half; and when he shall have accomplished to scatter the power of the holy people, all these things shall be finished.... Many shall be purified, and made white, and tried;* but the wicked shall do wickedly: and none of the wicked shall understand; but the wise shall understand. (Daniel 12:6, 7, 10, emphasis added)

---

[34] Ellen White stated repeatedly that Armageddon is the final battle for the hearts and minds of humanity under the outpouring of the latter rain. For more on that, see my book *The Final Atonement*.

At the commencement of Christ's ministry, when He was baptized, the Father spoke from above the Jordan River, and the Spirit descended and remained on Christ, anointing Him for His work. In the same way, when Christ takes the oath on behalf of His remnant people, He speaks from above the river flanked by the two holy ones, empowering the church with His Spirit (see Dan. 12:5ff; Rev. 10:1–11; 11:1–13).

Shortly before His crucifixion, Christ took three of His closest disciples with Him to a mountain where He was glorified and transfigured before them in the presence of Moses and Elijah, who flanked Him on either side. This scene parallels the two visions of Daniel 12 and Revelation 11, where, in both cases, two holy ones stand with Christ. At His transfiguration, the Father testified for the second time that Christ was truly His Son and commanded His people to hear and obey Him.

In linking the transfiguration of Christ with the two witnesses and His oath, inspiration gives us the assurance that Christ, our Prince, will be glorified once again during the final crisis in the same way the glory of God was revealed most majestically at the cross. Just as Christ, at His transfiguration, conversed with Moses and Elijah and was strengthened to endure the final trial awaiting Him, similarly, the oath He makes in the presence of the two witnesses is our assurance that Christ will be with His people at every step of the crisis until their work is finished and prophetic time ends.

In the last crisis, the church will be privileged to look on Him whom she has pierced and mourn for Him as for an only son (see Zech. 12:10). A primary means of the church capturing that vision is by participating in His sufferings. We will be baptized with the baptism. Many shall be purified and made white and tried (see Dan. 12:10).

As painful as the ordeal may be at times, it will be well worth it. The mystery of God, Christ in us, will be a reality (see Col. 1:27). The new covenant will be ratified in us—God's image restored. This is the promised seal of God, and it is worthy of our best efforts. All our works are wrought in God as we abide in Him. Praise God for His goodness, mercy, and miraculous transforming power.

Now notice in both Daniel 12 and Revelation 10, the power of the holy people will be scattered for a certain period. Regarding the oath and its meaning, the Spirit of Prophecy has this to say:

> This time, which the angel declares with a solemn oath, is not the end of this world's history, neither of probationary time, but of prophetic

time, which should precede the advent of our Lord. (White, *Manuscript Releases*, vol. 19, p. 320)

The scattering or breaking of the power of the holy people in Daniel 11 is the same event as the silencing of the two witnesses at the end of the 1,260 days in Revelation 11. The final warning of the two witnesses is also symbolized by the message of the three angels of Revelation 14, when the beast that ascends from the bottomless pit silences the two witnesses by the abomination of desolation.

The oath of Christ not only assures us that the mystery of God will be completed in us; it also promises that once the scattering and silencing of the holy people occurs, it will not be long before Christ returns. His assurance, given in both of the oaths, is given again: "The second woe is past; and, behold, the third woe cometh quickly" (Rev. 11:14).

At the third woe, God restores the kingdom and throne of David to His Son. Christ takes His great power, returns in splendor to the earth, joyfully rewards His people with immortality and crowns of victory, and reigns forever with them as King of kings and Lord of lords (see 2 Thess. 2:8; Rev. 19:11–16).

Chapter 28

Preparing for the Latter Rain

There is a growing awareness among Christians generally that the seven seals, seven trumpets, seven thunders, and seven plagues—the bulk of Revelation's prophecies, as well as Daniel's—are about to be fulfilled.

The concern among some Christians, and it is a valid concern, is these prophecies contain time elements, and that can be a lightning rod for people who are inclined to setting dates. There is always the risk with any movement, religious or secular, that some people will take things to extremes, but we can't let that blind us to the prophecies God has revealed. Time prophecies related to the future of God's people have been given from the earliest times and throughout sacred history.

The ministry of Christ was a prophetic fulfillment of the time prophecy of Daniel 9. Christ Himself told the disciples to preach, "The time is fulfilled and the kingdom of God is at hand" (Mark 1:15). Their message was time-sensitive but not time-focused. The focus was the call to repent and accept the Messiah as their Savior from sin, and this was undergirded by the time prophecies of Daniel 9.

I have suggested before that prophetic time ends when the testimony of the two witnesses is completed and they are "slain." Their message, like in Christ's day, is time-sensitive but will time itself be a test of faith? No.

At Pentecost, those in the upper room didn't know the exact time of the outpouring of the early rain; they were simply told by our Lord to wait for it. Similarly, there is going to be another important prayer-and-revival meeting in the future (see Rev. 8:1–5) that will, through the intercession of Christ and the saints, bring on the latter rain.

As the church senses her weakness and vulnerability as she's about to enter upon her final ordeal, she will pour her heart out to God to be braced to endure. Regarding how widespread the movement will be and the exact format, we will have to wait and see, but the overall picture we have is intense intercession on the part of both Christ and the church.

Only about 100 of Christ's followers besides the apostles were in the upper room at Pentecost. This was because these individuals were the few who loved Christ supremely, and out of love, they gladly and promptly heeded His instructions to tarry in Jerusalem. They likely suspected the Holy Spirit would be given during the upcoming feast, but they had no assurance from Christ that that was the case. During the period leading up to Pentecost, the realization took hold on this core group that their part was to humble themselves and press together in love and unity so they would personally and corporately be ready for the divine presence of the Comforter.

As we face the impending final conflict, that is our work today. The Lord would greatly bless His people if we followed this precedent:

> Then they that feared the LORD spake often one to another: and the LORD hearkened, and heard *it*, and a book of remembrance was written before him for them that feared the LORD, and that thought upon his name. And they shall be mine, saith the LORD of hosts, in that day when I make up my jewels; and I will spare them, as a man spareth his own son that serveth him. Then shall ye return, and discern between the righteous and the wicked, between him that serveth God and him that serveth him not. (Malachi 3:16–18)

Conclusion

> And he said unto me, These sayings are faithful and true: and the Lord God of the holy prophets sent his angel to shew unto his servants the things which must shortly be done. Behold, I come quickly: blessed is he that keepeth the sayings of the prophecy of this book.... I Jesus have sent mine angel to testify unto you these things in the churches. I am the root and the offspring of David, and the bright and morning star. And the Spirit and the bride say, Come. And let him that heareth say, Come. And let him that is athirst come. And whosoever will, let him take the water of life freely. (Revelation 22:6, 7, 16, 17)

For behold the stone that I have laid before Joshua; upon one stone *shall be* seven eyes: behold, I will engrave the graving thereof, saith the LORD of hosts, and I will remove the iniquity of that land in one day. In that day, saith the LORD of hosts, shall ye call every man his neighbour under the vine and under the fig tree. (Zechariah 3:9, 10)

Notice in the above verses that the iniquity of Israel will be removed in a single day: the Day of Atonement. Notice further what the results will be: the evangelization of the world! Once the sins of Joshua the high priest, a symbol of the Israel of God, are removed, he is given the commission of a priest-king. Immediately afterward, we see the two anointed witnesses and the seven blazing lamps.

> **"** Friends, Christ is about to mount His white horse and lead His mighty army to victory. The best days of the church are straight ahead. **"**

Friends, Christ is about to mount His white horse and lead His mighty army to victory. The best days of the church are straight ahead.

And I saw heaven opened, and behold a white horse; and he that sat upon him was called Faithful and True, and in righteousness he doth judge and make war. His eyes were as a flame of fire, and on his head were many crowns; And the armies which were in heaven followed him upon white horses, clothed in fine linen, white and clean. And he hath on his vesture and on his thigh a name written, KING OF KINGS, AND LORD OF LORDS. And I saw the beast, and the kings of the earth, and their armies, gathered together to make war against him that sat on the horse, and against his army. And the beast was taken, and with him the false prophet that wrought miracles before him, with which he deceived them that had received the mark of the beast, and them that worshipped his image. These both were cast alive into a lake of fire burning with brimstone. (Revelation 19:11–20)

He which testifieth these things saith, *Surely I come quickly.* Amen. Even so, come Lord Jesus. (Revelation 22:20, emphasis added)

Appendix A

The Sanctuary Doctrine by J.N. Andrews

One of the foremost nineteenth-century expositors of the sanctuary was John N. Andrews. The following twelve paragraphs are a condensed excerpt from his article "The Sanctuary" in the October 22, 1874, issue of *The Signs of the Times*:

> The Bible doctrine of the sanctuary is this: That the sanctuary is the place where the High Priest stands to offer blood before God for the sins of those who come to God through him. The central object in the sanctuary is the ark which contains the law of God that man has broken. The cover of this ark was called the mercy-seat, because mercy came to those who had broken the law beneath it, when the High priest sprinkled the blood of sin-offering upon it, provided he accompanied his work by repentance and faith. Last of all was the work of cleansing the sanctuary when the high priest by blood removed the sins of the people from the sanctuary into which they had been borne by the ministration of the priests before God. We now invite attention to the testimony of the Bible respecting the sanctuary.
>
> 1. There are two covenants; the first, or old covenant, extends from the time of Moses to the death of Christ; the second, or new covenant, begins at the death of Christ and extends forward to the consummation. Gal. 4:24–26; Heb. 8:7–13; Luke 22:20.
> 2. The first covenant had a sanctuary, which was the tabernacle erected by Moses. Heb. 9:1–17.

3. The new covenant has a sanctuary which is the temple of God in Heaven, into which our High Priest entered when he ascended upon high. Heb. 8:1–5.
4. When Moses erected the tabernacle, he was commanded by God to make it according to the pattern which he showed to him; and this pattern must have been a representation of the temple of God in Heaven; for the earthly sanctuary is declared to be a pattern of the heavenly. Ex. 25:9, 40; Heb. 8:5; 9:23....

The word sanctuary in the Bible, except in the few cases where it is used figuratively, refers always to the place in which the high priests ministers before God for the sins of the people. It was first the tabernacle erected by Moses; then it was the temple built by Solomon, which was a more glorious structure than the tabernacle, but with the same two holy places; and when the typical sacrifices ended in the death of Christ, who is the true sin offering, the earthly sanctuary, or, holy 'places', ceased to be the center of God's worship, and Christ entered the temple in Heaven as a great High Priest—"the minister of the sanctuary and of the true tabernacle, which the Lord, pitched, and not man." Heb 8:2. The temple of God in Heaven is the sanctuary from which the psalmist says the Lord beheld the earth (Ps. 102:19), and which Jeremiah speaks of as being where the throne of God is found. Jer. 17:12; Rev. 16:17.

The ministration in the earthly sanctuary could not actually take away sins; for it had only the blood of bulls and goats to offer. Heb. 10:4. It was given to Israel for the purpose of instructing them with reference to the work of Christ, and of encouraging them to look forward to his work. It is a shadow or representation of the service of Christ in the sanctuary of God in Heaven. Heb. 8:5; 10: 1; Col. 2:17. It took one year to complete the round of service in the earthly sanctuary, at the end of which the cleansing of the sanctuary took place. The round of service was repeated each year, even as a shadow is renewed each day. But the ministration of Christ which casts this shadow fills out each part of the work once for all, and is not repeated....

It is certain, therefore, that just as there was a time each year devoted to the finishing up of the round of service in "the example and shadow of heavenly things" so there is also such a period in the conclusion of Christ's ministration, when once for all our High Priest finishes his work of priesthood; and as this work in the former dispensation took place in the second apartment, so also under the New Covenant does this work find its accomplishment within the second veil by the ark of the ten commandments....

The work within the second apartment was for the cleansing of the sanctuary, and this was performed by the high priest with blood, and when it was accomplished the sins of the people were blotted out. It was, therefore, an event of the greatest importance to the people of God. The heavenly sanctuary is to be cleansed, and for the same reason that the earthly sanctuary was cleansed. So Paul testifies in Heb. 9:23.... The prophecy of Daniel 8:14 shows us that the sanctuary of God is cleansed in the last days of the New Covenant dispensation. The time marked for its cleansing is that fixed by John for the opening of the temple in Heaven and for the finishing of the mystery of God. Rev. 11:19; 10:7....

[T]he object of this final work in the sanctuary is to determine who are worthy of everlasting life... The investigation will determine who have overcome their sins; and these will have their sins blotted from the record, and their names retained in the book of life. It will also determine who have not overcome and these will have their names blotted from the book of life, Rev. 3:5, and their sins will be retained in the record, to be visited with retribution in the resurrection to damnation....

The righteous need a high priest until .their sins are blotted out. They cannot be blotted out till the Judgment; for God has decreed to bring every work into judgment whether good or evil. Eccl. 12:13, 14; 3:17. He certainly cannot bring any record into judgment after he has blotted it out. The blotting out is therefore the last act of our High Priest, and is done when the Father has accounted each person worthy of this; which will only be when the High Priest has shown from the record in the book of God's remembrance that he has actually overcome. The blotting out of sins (Acts 3:19) is therefore the great work which brings our Lord's priesthood to a conclusion. As this is an individual work, it evidently begins with the first generation of the righteous, and so comes down to the last, that is, to those who are alive at the coming of Christ. It is the time of the dead that they should be judged. Rev. 11:18, 19. The first -angel gives notice to the inhabitants of the earth that the hour of God's judgment has come. Rev. 14:6, 7. The living are still on probation when this solemn announcement is made to mankind.

The proclamation of the third angel, which is made while Christ is closing up his work in the sanctuary is designed to prepare the living for the decision of the Judgment. When the cases of the living are reached, [and fully judged] probation closes up forever. The decree goes forth from the throne of God, "He that is unjust, let him be unjust still and lie that is holy, let him be holy still." Rev. 22:11.

The sins of the overcomers being blotted out, and the sanctuary cleansed, the Son of God is no longer needed as a great High Priest. He therefore ceases from the office forever and becomes a king for the deliverance and glorification of his people, and for the destruction of all transgressors. Dan. 7:13, 14. Satan, the author of sin, receives its dreadful burden when the work in the sanctuary is closed, and will bear it with him to the lake of fire.

It is of infinite consequence to us who live in the time when Christ is closing up his priesthood, that we understand the work which he is performing, and that we so walk in the light as to share in his great salvation. J. N. ANDREWS.

Appendix B

How to Study Ezekiel's Temple

One reason many people shrink from an in-depth study of this vision is that the first three chapters are a detailed description of the layout, and to grasp the layout requires physically drawing it, which, unless you're an architect or engineer, is unfamiliar territory for most people. However, when the Lord told Ezekiel three times to document these measurements and show them to the people, did the Lord know what He was doing?

Of course He did. The One who created and endowed us with our mental capabilities invites us to come boldly to the throne of grace, and to help us, He has drawn out the map. Studying it is well worth the effort.

I am not an architect or a cartographer, but I've drawn out Ezekiel's temple many times, and every time, I learn something new. Instead of dreading the effort, think 'This'll be fun,' and you'll find it is a rewarding experience, albeit a bit awkward in the beginning.

I confess that when I first began studying this, I sometimes wondered if it was worth the effort, but the Spirit kept convicting me that this temple contained a goldmine of truth and mining it would pay rich dividends. It has for me. One of the best life choices I've ever made was my decision to be persistent and seek God for a better understanding of this.

Appendix C is a recent sketch I made of the basic layout. I've left out the dimensions and some details to keep it uncluttered, but the dimensions were the single most important element of the description in understanding the overall layout. If the dimensions didn't add up, I knew my layout was wrong. Because of their good fit, I have a high degree of confidence in the main elements, but as I said before, with each drawing, I learn something new.

I don't think I'm unique. Every time people prayerfully make the exertion to understand God's Word, they have a Divine Helper who ensures they learn some valuable spiritual lesson from it, not the least of which is patience and persistence. Those who do make the effort to grasp the layout will find themselves better able to understand the meaning of its laws and services. The layout, combined with the laws, help explain the atonement of the Prince, and this is our ultimate goal. We want to know how to cooperate with Christ so that the glory of the Lord—His character—will abide with us.

> Do a thorough comparative examination of all three sanctuaries: the Levitical tabernacle, the temple revealed to David, and Ezekiel's. All three interpret one another, and by carefully noting the differences between their structures, entrances and exits, and feasts and services, we come to a better understanding of sacred history—past and future, typified by the feasts—and our appreciation grows for the heavenly sanctuary, the blood that saves us, and the royal priesthood of our Prince.

Another tip for personal study is to do a thorough comparative examination of all three sanctuaries: the Levitical tabernacle, the temple revealed to David, and Ezekiel's. All three interpret one another, and by carefully noting the differences between their structures, entrances and exits, and feasts and services, we come to a better understanding of sacred history—past and future, typified by the feasts—and our appreciation grows for the heavenly sanctuary, the blood that saves us, and the royal priesthood of our Prince.

Appendix C
Layout of Ezekiel's Temple

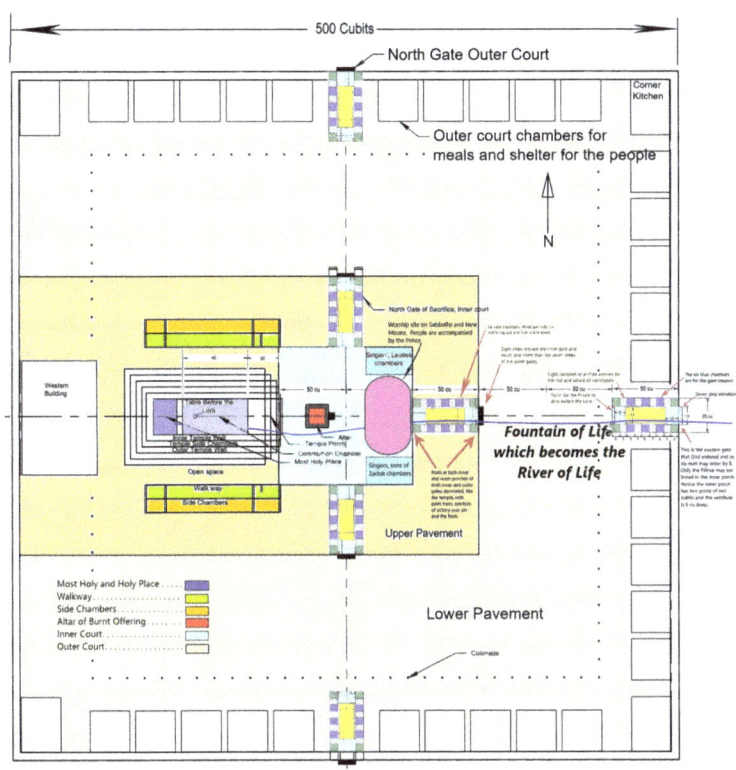

To view this chart at a higher resolution, go to: https://1ref.us/mset6

Appendix D

Table Comparing Burnt Offerings

The Levitical Corporate Offerings Compared to Ezekiel's Temple:

Corporate Worship and Feast Days	Calendar Date	Levitical	Ezekiel's Temple
Daily Burnt Offering also called the Continual Burnt Offering.	Every Day	Two male yearling lambs with a tenth ephah of flour mingled with a quarter hin of oil and a quarter hin of strong wine poured before the Lord. One lamb offered in the morning and the other in the evening. Num 28:3-8.	One male lamb with a sixth ephah of flour and a third of a hin of oil. **Offered in the morning only. No wine libation.*** Called the continual offering. Eze 46:14, 15.
Sabbath Burnt Offering and Sin Offering.	Every Sabbath	Same as above – two male lambs with their offerings. Num 28:9-10.	**One ram and six lambs, the ram with an ephah** of flour with a hin of oil and for the lambs a gift of flour as he is able with a hin of oil per ephah. Eze 46:4-5.

Table Comparing Burnt Offerings

Corporate Worship and Feast Days	Calendar Date	Levitical	Ezekiel's Temple
New Moon Burnt Offering and Sin Offering.	The first day of each month reckoned by the new moon. (The first month of the year was reckoned as the first new moon after the spring equinox.)	Two bulls, one ram and seven lambs with a thee tenths ephah flour per bull, two per ram and one per lamb. The oil is implied in the same proportions – a tenth ephah flour to a quarter hin of oil. The wine is half a hin per bull, a third per ram and a quarter per lamb. Also a goat for a sin offering. Not a Sabbath. Num 28:11-15.	**One bull, one ram and six male lambs** with one ephah per bull and per ram and for the lambs as he gives a gift with a hin of oil per ephah. **But no sin offering**. Notice the similarity to the Sabbath offering in Ezekiel's model, the difference being the addition of a bull. This implies a similarity between the New Moon and the Sabbath, both units of time. Eze 46:6-7.
Week of Atonement burnt offering and sin offering and atonement offering.	The 1st to the 7th day of the first month	Not observed.	No corporate burnt offering. Only the national sin offering on the 1st and seventh days of a **bull. No goat sin offering. Not a Sabbath.** Notice this atonement is similar to the Passover offering in this temple. The blood is applied to the posts of the temple, the ledge of the altar and inner court. Eze 45:18-20.
Passover Offering.	The evening of the 14th day of the first month	No corporate burnt offering except the daily continual offering. The Passover lamb was unique in that it wasn't a sin offering for the nation (a goat) but was for each household.	**A single bull is used for a national Passover offering, the blood applied to the posts of the temple, the bronze altar and inner court.** Eze 45:21, 22.

Corporate Worship and Feast Days	Calendar Date	Levitical	Ezekiel's Temple
Feast of Unleavened Bread Burnt and Sin Offerings and Sabbaths.	The 15th to the 21st day of the first month.	The burnt offering is the same as New Moon – all seven days – two bulls, one ram, seven lambs. Goat sin offering. First and last days are Sabbaths. Numbers 28:17-25	**Seven bulls and seven rams, all with one ephah and one hin of oil. One bull for sin offering. No Sabbaths.** Eze 45:21-24.
Feast of First Fruits Burnt & Sin Offering	The 16th day of the first month	Same as New Moon and Passover week. Numbers 28:26. A Sabbath.	Not observed.
Feast of Weeks or Pentecost Burnt, Sin and Peace Offerings compared.	The 50th day from First Fruits, the 66th day of the year.	One (rather than two) bull, one ram and seven male lambs with their grain and drink offerings. Also a goat sin offering. Also two male lambs for a peace offering that are holy to the Lord for the priests. Leviticus 23:15-21. A Sabbath. Notice, all the festive burnt offerings until now have two bulls, one ram and seven lambs. At this feast the number of bulls is reduced to one and this pattern is followed to the end of the year with the exception of the Feast of Tabernacles.	Not observed.
Feast of Trumpets Burnt and Sin Offerings.	The 1st day of the seventh month	One rather than two bulls, one ram and seven lambs. Same flour, oil and wine. Goat sin offering. Num 29:1-6. A Sabbath.	Not observed.

Table Comparing Burnt Offerings

Corporate Worship and Feast Days	Calendar Date	Levitical	Ezekiel's Temple
Day of Atonement Burnt, Sin and Atonement Off's.	The 10th day of the seventh month	Same as Trumpets and Pentecost. Goat for sin offering in addition to the sin offering of the atonement. Num 29:7-11. A Sabbath.	Not observed.
Feast of Tabernacles, Booths or Harvest Burnt and Sin Offerings and Sabbaths Compared.	The 15th to the 22st day of the seventh month. However in Ezekiel's temple the feast is a second Passover week and runs from the 15th to the 21st of the seventh month.	13 bulls, two rams and seven lambs for seven days. The first and eighth days are Sabbaths. The bulls diminished by one each day so that on the seventh day the burnt offering is seven bullocks, two rams and seven lambs with one goat for a sin offering. On the eighth day the burnt offering reverts to the same offering on Pentecost, Trumpets and the Day of Atonement, one bull, one ram and seven lambs with a goat for a sin offering Num 29:12-38.	**Seven bulls and seven rams with one bull for a for a sin offering. No Sabbaths.** Eze. 45:25.

*The main changes in Ezekiel's temple are bolded.

Appendix E

Selected Texts on the Day of the Lord

Behold, the day of the LORD comes, cruel, with wrath and fierce anger, to make the land a desolation and to destroy its sinners from it. For the stars of the heavens and their constellations will not give their light; the sun will be dark at its rising, and the moon will not shed its light. I will punish the world for its evil, and the wicked for their iniquity; I will put an end to the pomp of the arrogant, and lay low the pompous pride of the ruthless. I will make people more rare than fine gold, and mankind than the gold of Ophir. Therefore I will make the heavens tremble, and the earth will be shaken out of its place, at the wrath of the LORD of hosts in the day of his fierce anger. (Isaiah 13:9–13)

Behold, the LORD will empty the earth and make it desolate, and he will twist its surface and scatter its inhabitants. And it shall be, as with the people, so with the priest; as with the slave, so with his master; as with the maid, so with her mistress; as with the buyer, so with the seller; as with the lender, so with the borrower; as with the creditor, so with the debtor.... The wasted city is broken down; every house is shut up so that none can enter. There is an outcry in the streets for lack of wine; all joy has grown dark; the gladness of the earth is banished. Desolation is left in the city; the gates are battered into ruins.... Terror and the pit and the snare are upon you, O inhabitant of the earth! He who flees at the sound of the terror shall fall into the pit, and he who climbs out of the pit shall be caught in the snare. For the windows of heaven are opened, and the foundations of the earth tremble. The earth is utterly broken, the earth is split apart, the earth is violently shaken. The earth staggers like a drunken man; it sways like a hut; its transgression lies heavy upon it, and it falls, and will not rise again. (Isaiah 24:1, 2, 10–12, 17–20)

Behold, the name of the LORD comes from afar, burning with his anger, and in thick rising smoke; his lips are full of fury, and his tongue is like a devouring fire; his breath is like an overflowing stream that reaches up to the neck; to sift the nations with the sieve of destruction, and to place on the jaws of the peoples a bridle that leads astray. You shall have a song as in the night when a holy feast is kept, and gladness of heart, as when one sets out to the sound of the flute to go to the mountain of the LORD, to the Rock of Israel. And the LORD will cause his majestic voice to be heard and the descending blow of his arm to be seen, in furious anger and a flame of devouring fire, with a cloudburst and storm and hailstones. The Assyrians will be terror-stricken at the voice of the LORD, when he strikes with his rod. And every stroke of the appointed staff that the LORD lays on them will be to the sound of tambourines and lyres. Battling with brandished arm, he will fight with them. For a burning place has long been prepared; indeed, for the king it is made ready, its pyre made deep and wide, with fire and wood in abundance; the breath of the LORD, like a stream of sulfur, kindles it. (Isaiah 30:27–33)

The mountains quake at Him, and the hills melt, and the earth is burned at His presence, yea, the world, and all that dwell therein. Who can stand before His indignation? and who can abide in the fierceness of His anger? His fury is poured out like fire, and the rocks are thrown down by Him. (Nahum 1:5, 6)

Bow thy heavens, O Lord, and come down: touch the mountains, and they shall smoke. Cast forth lightning, and scatter them: shoot out thine arrows, and destroy them. (Psalm 144:5, 6)

As I looked, thrones were placed, and the Ancient of Days took his seat; his clothing was white as snow, and the hair of his head like pure wool; his throne was fiery flames; its wheels were burning fire. A stream of fire issued and came out from before him; a thousand thousands served him, and ten thousand times ten thousand stood before him; the court sat in judgment, and the books were opened. (Daniel 7:9, 10)

And I will show wonders in the heavens and on the earth, blood and fire and columns of smoke. The sun shall be turned to darkness, and the moon to blood, before the great and awesome day of the LORD comes. And it shall come to pass that everyone who calls on the name of the LORD shall be saved. For in Mount Zion and in Jerusalem there shall be those who escape, as the LORD has said, and among the survivors shall be those whom the LORD calls. (Joel 2:30–32)

God came from Teman, and the Holy One from Mount Paran. Selah. His splendor covered the heavens, and the earth was full of his praise. His brightness was like the light; rays flashed from his hand; and there he veiled his power. Before him went pestilence, and plague followed at his heels [Reminds you of COVID, doesn't it?]. He stood and measured the earth; he looked and shook the nations; then the eternal mountains were scattered; the everlasting hills sank low. His were the everlasting ways. I saw the tents of Cushan in affliction; the curtains of the land of Midian did tremble.... The mountains saw you and writhed; the raging waters swept on; the deep gave forth its voice; it lifted its hands on high [Expect major tsunamis with this seismic activity]. The sun and moon stood still in their place at the light of your arrows as they sped, at the flash of your glittering spear. You marched through the earth in fury; you threshed the nations in anger. You went out for the salvation of your people, for the salvation of your anointed. You crushed the head of the house of the wicked, laying him bare from thigh to neck. Selah. (Habakkuk 3:3–7, 10–13)

When he opened the sixth seal, I looked, and behold, there was a great earthquake, and the sun became black as sackcloth, the full moon became like blood, and the stars of the sky fell to the earth as the fig tree sheds its winter fruit when shaken by a gale [Note: After this seal is broken, the 144,000 are sealed]. (Revelation 6:12, 13)

Appendix F

Ellen White's First Vision

While I was praying at the family altar, the Holy Ghost fell upon me, and I seemed to be rising higher and higher, far above the dark world. I turned to look for the Advent people in the world, but could not find them, when a voice said to me, "Look again, and look a little higher." At this I raised my eyes, and saw a straight and narrow path, cast up high above the world. On this path the Advent people were traveling to the city, which was at the farther end of the path. They had a bright light set up behind them at the beginning of the path, which an angel told me was the midnight cry. This light shone all along the path and gave light for their feet so that they might not stumble. If they kept their eyes fixed on Jesus, who was just before them, leading them to the city, they were safe. But soon some grew weary, and said the city was a great way off, and they expected to have entered it before. Then Jesus would encourage them by raising His glorious right arm, and from His arm came a light which waved over the Advent band, and they shouted, "Alleluia!" Others rashly denied the light behind them and said that it was not God that had led them out so far. The light behind them went out, leaving their feet in perfect darkness, and they stumbled and lost sight of the mark and of Jesus, and fell off the path down into the dark and wicked world below. Soon we heard the voice of God like many waters, which gave us the day and hour of Jesus' coming. The living saints, 144,000 in number, knew and understood the voice, while the wicked thought it was thunder and an earthquake. When God spoke the time, He poured upon us the Holy Ghost, and our faces began to light up and shine with the glory of God, as Moses' did when he came down from Mount Sinai.

The 144,000 were all sealed and perfectly united. On their foreheads was written, God, New Jerusalem, and a glorious star containing Jesus' new name. At our happy, holy state the wicked were enraged, and would rush violently up to lay hands on us to thrust us into prison, when we would stretch forth the hand in the name of the Lord, and they would fall helpless to the ground. Then it was that the synagogue of Satan knew that God had loved us who could wash one another's feet and salute the brethren with a holy kiss, and they worshiped at our feet.

Soon our eyes were drawn to the east, for a small black cloud had appeared, about half as large as a man's hand, which we all knew was the sign of the Son of man. We all in solemn silence gazed on the cloud as it drew nearer and became lighter, glorious, and still more glorious, till it was a great white cloud. The bottom appeared like fire; a rainbow was over the cloud, while around it were ten thousand angels, singing a most lovely song; and upon it sat the Son of man. His hair was white and curly and lay on His shoulders; and upon His head were many crowns. His feet had the appearance of fire; in His right hand was a sharp sickle; in His left, a silver trumpet. His eyes were as a flame of fire, which searched His children through and through. Then all faces gathered paleness, and those that God had rejected gathered blackness. Then we all cried out, "Who shall be able to stand? Is my robe spotless?" Then the angels ceased to sing, and there was some time of awful silence, when Jesus spoke: "Those who have clean hands and pure hearts shall be able to stand; My grace is sufficient for you." At this our faces lighted up, and joy filled every heart. And the angels struck a note higher and sang again, while the cloud drew still nearer the earth.

Then Jesus' silver trumpet sounded, as He descended on the cloud, wrapped in flames of fire. He gazed on the graves of the sleeping saints, then raised His eyes and hands to heaven, and cried, "Awake! awake! awake! ye that sleep in the dust, and arise." Then there was a mighty earthquake. The graves opened, and the dead came up clothed with immortality. The 144,000 shouted, "Alleluia!" as they recognized their friends who had been torn from them by death, and in the same moment we were changed and caught up together with them to meet the Lord in the air.

We all entered the cloud together, and were seven days ascending to the sea of glass, when Jesus brought the crowns, and with His own right hand placed them on our heads. He gave us harps of gold and palms of victory. Here on the sea of glass the 144,000 stood in a perfect square. Some of them had very bright crowns, others not so bright. Some crowns appeared heavy with stars, while others had but few. All were perfectly satisfied with their crowns. And they were all clothed with a glorious white mantle from their shoulders to their feet. Angels were all about us as we marched over the sea of glass to the gate of the city. Jesus raised His mighty, glorious arm, laid hold of the pearly gate, swung it back on its glittering hinges, and said to us, "You have washed your robes in My blood, stood stiffly for My truth, enter in." We all marched in and felt that we had a perfect right in the city.

Here we saw the tree of life and the throne of God. Out of the throne came a pure river of water, and on either side of the river was the tree of life. On one side of the river was a trunk of a tree, and a trunk on the other side of the river, both of pure, transparent gold. At first I thought I saw two trees. I looked again, and saw that they were united at the top in one tree. So it was the tree of life on either side of the river of life. Its branches bowed to the place where we stood, and the fruit was glorious; it looked like gold mixed with silver.

We all went under the tree and sat down to look at the glory of the place, when Brethren Fitch and Stockman, who had preached the gospel of the kingdom, and whom God had laid in the grave to save them, came up to us and asked us what we had passed through while they were sleeping. We tried to call up our greatest trials, but they looked so small compared with the far more exceeding and eternal weight of glory that surrounded us that we could not speak them out, and we all cried out, "Alleluia, heaven is cheap enough!" and we touched our glorious harps and made heaven's arches ring.

With Jesus at our head we all descended from the city down to this earth, on a great and mighty mountain, which could not bear Jesus up, and it parted asunder, and there was a mighty plain. Then we looked up and saw the great city, with twelve foundations, and twelve gates, three on each side, and an angel at each gate. We all cried out, "The city, the great city, it's coming, it's coming down from God out of heaven," and it came and settled on the place where we stood. Then we began to look at the glorious things outside of the city. There I saw most glorious houses, that had the appearance of silver, supported by four pillars set with pearls most glorious to behold. These were to be inhabited by the saints. In each was a golden shelf. I saw many of the saints go into the houses, take off their glittering crowns and lay them on the shelf, then go out into the field by the houses to do something with the earth; not as we have to do with the earth here; no, no. A glorious light shone all about their heads, and they were continually shouting and offering praises to God.

I saw another field full of all kinds of flowers, and as I plucked them, I cried out, "They will never fade." Next I saw a field of tall grass, most glorious to behold; it was living green and had a reflection of silver and gold, as it waved proudly to the glory of King Jesus. Then we entered a field full of all kinds of beasts—the lion, the lamb, the leopard, and the wolf, all together in perfect union. We passed through the midst of them, and they followed on peaceably after. Then we entered a wood, not like the dark woods we have here; no, no; but light, and all over glorious; the branches of the trees moved to and fro, and we all cried out, "We will dwell safely in the wilderness and sleep in the woods." We passed through the woods, for we were on our way to Mount Zion.

As we were traveling along, we met a company who also were gazing at the glories of the place. I noticed red as a border on their garments; their crowns were brilliant; their robes were pure white. As we greeted them, I asked Jesus who they were. He said they were martyrs that had been slain for Him. With them was an innumerable company of little ones; they also had a hem of red on their garments. Mount Zion was just before us, and on the mount was a glorious temple, and about it were seven other mountains, on which grew roses and lilies. And I saw the little ones climb, or, if they chose, use their little wings and fly, to the top of the mountains and pluck the never-fading flowers. There were all kinds of trees around the temple to beautify the place: the box, the pine, the fir, the oil, the myrtle, the pomegranate, and the fig tree bowed down with the weight of its timely figs—these made the place all over glorious. And as we were about to enter the holy temple, Jesus raised His lovely voice and said, "Only the 144,000 enter this place," and we shouted, "Alleluia."

This temple was supported by seven pillars, all of transparent gold, set with pearls most glorious. The wonderful things I there saw I cannot describe. Oh, that I could talk in the language of Canaan, then could I tell a little of the glory of the better world. I saw there tables of stone in which the names of the 144,000 were engraved in letters of gold. After we beheld the glory of the temple, we went out, and Jesus left us and went to the city. Soon we heard His lovely voice again, saying, "Come, My people, you have come out of great tribulation, and done My will; suffered for Me; come in to supper, for I will gird Myself, and serve you." We shouted, "Alleluia! glory!" and entered into the city. And I saw a table of pure silver; it was many miles in length, yet our eyes could extend over it. I saw the fruit of the tree of life, the manna, almonds, figs, pomegranates, grapes, and many other kinds of fruit. I asked Jesus to let me eat of the fruit. He said, "Not now. Those who eat of the fruit of this land go back to earth no more. But in a little while, if faithful, you shall both eat of the fruit of the tree of life and drink of the water of the fountain." And

He said, "You must go back to the earth again and relate to others what I have revealed to you." Then an angel bore me gently down to this dark world. Sometimes I think I can stay here no longer; all things of earth look so dreary. I feel very lonely here, for I have seen a better land. Oh, that I had wings like a dove, then would I fly away and be at rest! (*Early Writings*, pp. 14–19)

Appendix G

The Covenant and the Mosaic Code

Freedom of Conscience in Ancient Israel

In the days and years after 9/11, Americans willingly sacrificed much of their privacy and personal liberty for the sake of national security. Today, over two decades later, America is well down the path of repudiating what is left of its Constitution, sacrificing its protection of freedom of conscience on the altars of political correctness and extreme views on hot button issues such as the environment, transgenderism, and public health.

How did we get here as a nation? Besides fearmongering, a major factor is that for many years, a majority of America's religious leaders, Christian and Jewish, have more or less rejected the Ten Commandments and the God of the Old Testament. As a result, the American mind has no barrier to adopting a false worldview and moral standard.

However, the New Testament writers and Christ Himself were equally clear that the God of the New Testament is also the God of the Old. He does not change. All Scripture is equally inspired, including the laws and statutes of Moses, of which Christ said, "If they hear not Moses and the prophets, neither will they be persuaded, though one rose from the dead" (Luke 16:31).

That saying of Christ was proved true just days after He made it. As He was about to enter Jerusalem seated on a donkey, led by Lazarus,[35] who he had just recently raised from the dead, the Jewish leaders denied the

---
[35] See White, *The Desire of Ages*, p. 572.

testimony of Lazarus and the crowd who acknowledged Christ as Israel's king. A few days later, Christ was crucified for the common good of the people, according to the mindset of the high priest, Caiaphas.

Caiaphas was wrongly right; Christ did die for the common good, but to Caiaphas, it was not that Christ's life had redeeming value but that the national interest trumped the life of one humble Galilean. The same human wisdom and argument for the common good is being used now in both the secular and religious sectors of America.

> *Caiaphas was wrongly right; Christ did die for the common good, but to Caiaphas, it was not that Christ's life had redeeming value but that the national interest trumped the life of one humble Galilean. The same human wisdom and argument for the common good is being used now in both the secular and religious sectors of America.*

In Scripture, the question is asked, "If the foundations be destroyed, what can the righteous do?" (Ps. 11:3). The underpinning of society is a sensitive national conscience that understands the issues of justice and equity, but what is justice? Justice and mercy, according to Scripture, is doing right by all, including and especially those who are weakest and powerless to defend themselves. This standard of right-doing is defined by the law of God (see Isa. 58:6–12; Mic. 6:8; Exod. 23:1–9).

It is no coincidence that at the time when America is marginalizing the best elements of its society by demonizing those who are moral, it is also at the height of its war on the unborn. Both are at the mercy of an increasingly callous element that mistakes the bondage of lust and license for liberty and freedom.

In Scripture, freedom of conscience and religion does indeed look different from the current conceptions of it. For example, open idolatry was not allowed under Mosaic law:

> If there arise among you a prophet, or a dreamer of dreams, and giveth thee a sign or a wonder, And the sign or the wonder come to pass, whereof he spake unto thee, saying, Let us go after other gods, which thou hast not known, and let us serve them; Thou shalt not hearken unto the words of that prophet, or that dreamer of dreams: for the LORD your God proveth you, to know whether ye love the LORD your God with all your heart and with all your soul. And that prophet, or that dreamer of dreams, shall be put to death; because he hath spoken to turn you away from the LORD your God. (Deuteronomy 13:1–5)

The death penalty for propagating error and falsehood may seem extreme today, but this provision is the polar opposite of the current tyranny of our thought police culture. When one segment of society attempts to force all segments to call a biological male "her," we know we're in new territory: that our moral compass isn't working.

Contrast our current gender confusion with Deuteronomy 13, which has its counterpart in the gospel commission of Christ. Our commission is to proclaim truth, not lies and error. While Deuteronomy 13 prohibits propagating falsehood, the individual conscience is still free to choose. There is no provision in this chapter or anywhere else in Scripture for thought-policing and mandates forcing the conscience. Throughout the Bible, the only acceptable service to God is voluntary—springing from a willing heart.

We can see the principles of freedom and justice not only in the Mosaic law and the gospel, but also illustrated throughout Old Testament history. Under the rule of Israel's godly kings, the most enlightened concepts of freedom and justice prevailed. At the start of Solomon's reign, for example, two young harlots (young enough to bear children) came to him with two babies, one dead and the other living, disputing who gave birth to the living child.

Harlotry was and is illegal under both the Mosaic law and the seventh commandment. As these two women, neither with legal standing, petitioned Solomon, He could have taken the living child, placed him in "protective custody," and banished the women from the Holy City. Instead, he judged this case, restored the living child to the distraught mother, and imposed no penalty on the guilty harlot. He judged righteously between two harlots with no legal standing.

This was the Spirit of God in Solomon shining out of the law, showing the divine balance of mercy and justice. It was and is the glory of God to cover the sin of these unfortunate women, give them standing, hear their cause, and by this, give them another opportunity to repent and become loyal subjects of His kingdom. In heaven, we'll learn if either of them responded to the divine grace ministered through the Spirit manifesting wisdom in Solomon.

David, the man after God's own heart, told us what the source of his own wisdom was and the origin of his tender bond to God: He loved His laws, statutes, and judgments; he meditated on them day and night; and they were more precious to him than was his daily bread:

> O how love I thy law! it is my meditation all the day. Thou through thy commandments hast made me wiser than mine enemies: for

they are ever with me. I have more understanding than all my teachers: for thy testimonies are my meditation. I understand more than the ancients, because I keep thy precepts. I have refrained my feet from every evil way, that I might keep thy word. I have not departed from thy judgments: for thou hast taught me. How sweet are thy words unto my taste! yea, sweeter than honey to my mouth! Through thy precepts I get understanding: therefore I hate every false way. (Psalm 119:97–104)

How many of us share David's sentiments? If more of us truly loved the precepts and statutes of God as David did, more of us would be men and women after the heart of God. I want to be that, don't you? We can be by following the same course of careful, reverent study and practical application of these provisions. The same course will bring the same results.

The principles of the Mosaic law are timeless and hold their value into eternity, but we should have no illusion that they will ever be implemented in a fallen world in the end times, when the global rule of sin reaches its climax. It is the rejection of these principles by the man of sin that destroys the foundations of society. This is the abomination that makes the earth desolate; it is the slaying of the two witnesses, a process that is well underway today in Western culture.

On the boarders of the Promised Land, Moses, in his last address, admonished Israel to correctly value these provisions:

Behold, I have taught you statutes and judgments, even as the LORD my God commanded me, that ye should do so in the land whither ye go to possess it. Keep therefore and do *them*; for this *is* your wisdom and your understanding in the sight of the nations, which shall hear all these statutes, and say, Surely this great nation *is* a wise and understanding people. For what nation *is there so* great, who *hath* God *so* nigh unto them, as the LORD our God *is* in all *things that* we call upon him *for*? And what nation *is there so* great, that hath statutes and judgments *so* righteous as all this law, which I set before you this day? (Deuteronomy 4:5–8)

Let's take some time to meditate on that divine statement and let it sink deep into our souls. These provisions are part of that living bread and hidden manna with which God wants to nourish us.

Relevance of the Mosaic Code

A sound moral character is rooted in an individual's personal sense of justice and mercy. If we are mature spiritually, we should be able to say, like King David did, that we delight to do the will of God and His law is written within our hearts (see Ps. 40:8). If the divine law is internalized in us, we will be just and merciful as God is just and merciful.

Most Christians think of the law as the Ten Commandments, but in addition to these, there are many more statutes and judgments in the books of Moses that most Christians either don't know exist or dismiss as part of the ceremonial law.

The statutes of the Mosaic law (see Exod. 20:18–23:33), like the Ten Commandments, were also given by God and formed an integral part of the covenant between God and Israel. Like the Decalogue, they are to enlighten us as a lamp for our feet so we can adjust our thinking and conduct to the divine standard of righteousness. They are a valuable window into the practical application of the principles of the Ten Commandments.

Christians have been too quick to discard these, assuming they are part of the ceremonial law that was removed at the cross, but think about it for a moment. If these laws harmonized with the Ten Commandments when they were given, they did not cease to harmonize with it at the cross. The specific components that relate to the ceremonial law will, of course, not apply now, but there is little, in many of them, that is tied to the ceremonial system. To the extent they are not tied to it—and many are not—their principles are timeless.

When I was a young man attending law school in Canada (Queen's University, Kingston, Ontario) and being bombarded daily with human wisdom, I was often refreshed and enlightened by comparing modern notions of law and justice with these divine standards. The Mosaic law was like an oasis and a lens that allowed me to sort through the clamor of legal jargon and sophistry and enabled me to see the underlying issues more clearly. Forty years later, I find them as enlightening today as I did then—even more so.

Perhaps the greatest historical proof of the wisdom and soundness of the Mosaic code is the unprecedented power and prosperity Israel enjoyed under the reigns of David and Solomon. From the beginning of Israel's existence as a nation, these statutes and judgments, along with the Ten Commandments, formed the basis of the covenant agreement between it and God. These were the nation's divine legacy given to them by their King at Mount Sinai. As a nation, they were never to amend them because they could not be improved. They were only to implement them. However, for 400 years after the exodus, they repeatedly broke them and followed the laws and customs of their heathen neighbors—the same sad course followed today by the majority of Christians and Jews.

Finally, in David, God found a man after His own heart—one who would rule righteously, like Abraham did, who had commanded his household after him. David understood that the covenant code of Moses was to be the divine foundation of Israel's government and its source of greatness. From his youth, the Mosaic precepts were David's study, delight, and source of his wisdom, and when God exalted him to the throne, they formed the basis of his rule of equity and justice.

David's example of fidelity (notwithstanding his fall) was followed by Solomon during the first part of his reign, and the record states the glory of his rule overwhelmed the greatest of the earth's monarchs. The queen of Sheba was astounded; her spirit fainted in her, she said, when she beheld the glory of Solomon's reign; and she was left almost speechless (see 1 Kings 10:4, 5). Think for a moment of how different the history of the world and Israel would have been if Solomon and his descendants had *remained* true to this covenant and God, the Lawgiver.

Today, there is a certain urgency to this. Based on the current political trajectory, our days of peace and prosperity are numbered. Why? Because these provisions condemn the darkness that has overtaken Western society and the world. Before long, prophecy indicates the beast of Daniel and Revelation will impose another Hitler-style final solution: It will silence the two witnesses, slaying them (see Rev. 11).

However, to the arrogant who are hell-bent on this course, I would remind them that it is this standard of righteousness that is the foundation of society now and in the kingdom of God under the new covenant. If you replace these righteous laws with the counterfeit freedoms of lust, license, and perversion and pit one race against another to revenge the past, you destroy the foundations of society. Once the foundations are destroyed and the two witnesses are

> *If you replace these righteous laws with the counterfeit freedoms of lust, license, and perversion and pit one race against another to revenge the past, you destroy the foundations of society. Once the foundations are destroyed and the two witnesses are slain, there will be no remedy. Chaos will ensue. It has already begun. We have a taste of it in the riots and mass shootings that are becoming the norm.*

slain, there will be no remedy. Chaos will ensue. It has already begun. We have a taste of it in the riots and mass shootings that are becoming the norm.

Momentarily, we will look at these provisions in more detail and briefly consider the overall legal structure of the Mosaic code. As we do, keep in mind that we want to understand the spirit of the law, not merely the letter. By bowing in submission to the expressed will of God for individuals and society, we will find our highest freedom and greatest joy.

With that said, be warned; these statutes and ordinances will not always strike us as totally balanced, just, and merciful. If they did, there would be no need to study them. The reason they are written down for us is so we can adjust our thinking and conduct, which sin has corrupted, and bring every highhanded, rebellious thought into captivity to the will and wisdom of God. May He help us to cooperate with Christ so we may be sealed by Him under the new covenant, counted worthy to escape the perils of the last days, and stand before the Son of Man.

Overview of the Mosaic Code

In the following summary of the Mosaic code, after some brief commentary, I've listed all the major punishable acts in the law of Moses. I might have made this pill easier to swallow by first reviewing the many merciful provisions (e.g., those protecting widows, orphans, strangers, and slaves), but those don't lend themselves as readily to neat categories, so I may leave them for a later time.

The purpose of this list is to show the relative seriousness of all the major crimes according to inspiration, as well as the connection between the act and the corresponding punishment, which helps to give us a balanced, true understanding of sin, righteousness, mercy, and judgment. These precepts form an important part of the divine antidote to modern humanity's confused values.

To the modern mind, stoning, hanging, and burning are barbaric. While there's no doubt these are gruesome punishments, an unbiased mind will see in them a divine, merciful warning of what the transgressor will ultimately face: the undiluted wrath of God.[36] Scripture is consistent

---

[36] This wrath brings death, not eternal torment. Under God's just rule, the punishment always fits the crime. A finite crime by a finite being brings a finite punishment. "The wages of sin is death" (Rom. 6:23).

on this point: Those who sow to the wind will reap the whirlwind (see Hosea 8:7).

Under modern notions of "cruel and unusual punishment," any punishment that inflicts significant physical pain falls into the category of barbaric. This is conventional wisdom, yet as we've seen in recent years, it is no barrier to modern forms of cruelty. Consider, for example, how things have unfolded since 9/11 in America, with its use of torture to gather intelligence and gain confessions. For a time, our abhorrence of torture was pushed aside in the interest of the common good and national security. Fortunately, we have officially backed away from that after finding it is not effective. As we would expect, information gleaned from torture is unreliable and often worse than useless.

While physical pain is considered cruel and unusual today, emotional pain is not. Prisoners who misbehave and are often emotionally unstable are routinely isolated in solitary confinement for long periods. There is no precedent for or sanctioning of this in the Mosaic code. In contrast, the divine statutes provide that a brief dose of physical suffering for wrong conduct can be as effective in adults as it is in children, as long as it is administered equitably, in love, and as a last resort (see Deut. 25:1–3).

For the sake of easy comparison, the statutes listed below are arranged in four categories, from least to most serious. Although this list progresses from the lesser to the greater offenses, we should bear in mind that no sin is minor or inconsequential. Paradise was lost through a supposedly minor transgression: yielding to inordinate appetite through unbelief.

The first category includes culpable acts that merit monetary penalties or corporal stripes. It includes both lesser crimes and negligent acts. Notice that unlike the common law of Britain and America, the Mosaic code doesn't make a distinction between civil and criminal negligence but presents a balanced unity of both.

One punishment that is conspicuous by its absence from all the lesser crimes (and the greater) is incarceration. This is one of the greatest differences between the Mosaic code and modern law.

Another notable difference is while modern law removes the personal element of the crime against another person and substitutes a "debt to society" that is paid by the duration of the incarceration, the Mosaic code preserves the original connection between the parties as an important element of justice.

Mosaic law provides a seamless unity of both civil and criminal liability and does so without creating a vast penal system of incarceration: The person who causes disfigurement is punished in kind or pays damages.

The person who breaches a trust or breaks something borrowed is required to make it good. The thief is required to make direct restitution, in some cases either adding a fifth, doubling, or quintupling, depending on factors like the thief confessing voluntarily, property type, and if the original asset is returned. If the guilty party cannot make it good, he or she is to be sold as a bondservant for a maximum of seven years, and the money is used to satisfy the obligation.

Notwithstanding, notice the offender is still required to be a useful member of society. In no case is a person kept in idle confinement for years on end in the company of other idle inmates by whom the younger, weaker ones are often demoralized and victimized.

The second category is offenses that merit death by hanging. There are three of these, but they include the most common serious offenses: murder, negligence causing death, and kidnapping. This is one of the most instructive portions of the Mosaic law. In His wisdom, Israel's Lawgiver makes a clear distinction between neglect and evil intent. In the case of murder, which, like in contemporary law, must include evil intent, monetary compensation is not to be allowed or considered. The only permissible penalty for murder is death.

However, where evil intent is not present but negligence is a factor, monetary compensation is permissible. The divine distinction between fatal negligence and murder in itself should be of interest to anyone who is familiar with the common law legacy of Britain, which mirrors Scripture on this point quite well, the main difference being that the Mosaic law always preserves the direct connection between the perpetrator and the victim.

The third category covers offenses that merit death by stoning. There are seven of these.

The fourth category covers the most serious offenses that merit death by fire. There are only two, both of which are sexual, but these are aggravated beyond other sexual sins (see the third category) in that they are gross perversions that strike at the core pillars of society: the family and the priesthood.

Once this list is studied, in order to get a still better understanding of the justice and mercy of God, I recommend carefully reviewing these in the context of the other statutes and judgments of Scripture.

Also, the provisions for cities of refuge in cases of accidental death are instructive. Note how these provisions mesh seamlessly with the overall provisions for murder (see Num. 35:6–32).

Also noteworthy are the merciful provisions regarding the treatment of bondservants (see Exod. 21:2–6). All of these integrate seamlessly with the rest of the code and the divine plan for Israel as an agrarian nation of twelve distinct tribes and states with inalienable land rights that were preserved for all posterity by the sabbaticals and jubilees (see Lev. 25).

To round out your study, review the crimes or sins of neglect and failure to perform a positive duty that have no specific punishment and were matters of conscience: the sin by parents of neglecting to restrain children and teach them self-control (see Exod. 21:15–21; Prov. 22:6); the crime or sin of neglecting to educate children to love God and His law (see Deut. 4:9; 6:7); the sin of oppressing the poor and charging them interest (see Lev. 25:36, 37; Deut. 23:19, 20); the sin of failing to help our enemies when they are in need (see Exod. 23:4); and the crime of not defending the fatherless, widow, etc. (see Exod. 22:22–24; Deut. 24:17–21).

Truly, this was an unparalleled source of wisdom and continues to be so today. In the New Testament, the greatest discourse of Christ that expounds the spiritual nature of the law is the Sermon on the Mount (see Matt. 5–7). In studying the Mosaic code, we would also do well to bring to bear at the same time the applications of the law made by Christ.

For the diligent students and doers of the law, God says He will show us wonderful things out of it. His testimonies and statutes, like the beatitudes and sayings from Christ's mountain discourse, are a window that expands on the principles of the Decalogue. When these lesser statutes are prized above gold, they will be found to be sweeter than honey.

These have power to convert our souls, pointing out our transgression, steering us to righteousness, goodness, and love, and, in the process, making us wiser than our peers and the aged sage. The Word of God, both Old and New Testaments, is life for us. In giving due reverence to His commandments, judgments, testimonies, and statutes—in loving them and feeding on them—we will be nourished by every word that proceeds from the mouth of God.

Here is the list:

1. **Crimes and offenses meriting monetary compensation and/or stripes**

    Injuring a neighbor in a fight:

    > And if men strive together, and one smite another with a stone, or with *his* fist, and he die not, but keepeth *his* bed: If he rise again, and walk abroad upon his staff, then shall he that smote *him* be quit: only he shall pay *for* the loss of his time, and shall cause *him* to be thoroughly healed. And if a man smite his servant, or his maid, with a rod, and

he die under his hand; he shall be surely punished. Notwithstanding, if he continue a day or two, he shall not be punished: for he *is* his money. (Exodus 21:18–21)

Negligence causing property damage or loss:

And if a man shall open a pit, or if a man shall dig a pit, and not cover it, and an ox or an ass fall therein; The owner of the pit shall make it good, and give money unto the owner of them; and the dead beast shall be his. And if one man's ox hurt another's, that he die; then they shall sell the live ox, and divide the money of it; and the dead ox also they shall divide. Or if it be known that the ox hath used to push in time past, and his owner hath not kept him in; he shall surely pay ox for ox; and the dead shall be his own. (Exodus 21:33–36)

Injuring or causing the miscarriage of another man's wife because of a fight between the men:

If men strive, and hurt a woman with child, so that her fruit depart from her, and yet no mischief follow: he shall be surely punished, according as the woman's husband will lay upon him; and he shall pay as the judges determine. And if any mischief follow, then thou shalt give life for life, Eye for eye, tooth for tooth, hand for hand, foot for foot, Burning for burning, wound for wound, stripe for stripe. (Exodus 21:22–25)

Injuring a bondservant:

And if a man smite the eye of his servant, or the eye of his maid, that it perish; he shall let him go free for his eye's sake. And if he smite out his manservant's tooth, or his maidservant's tooth; he shall let him go free for his tooth's sake. (Exodus 21:26, 27)

Injustice between neighbors in disputes other than a physical fight:

If there be a controversy between men, and they come unto judgment, that the judges may judge them; then they shall justify the righteous, and condemn the wicked. And it shall be, if the wicked man be worthy to be beaten, that the judge shall cause him to lie down, and to be beaten before his face, according to his fault, by a certain number.

Forty stripes he may give him, and not exceed: lest, if he should exceed, and beat him above these with many stripes, then thy brother should seem vile unto thee. (Deuteronomy 25:1–3)

Theft of production assets:

If a man shall steal an ox, or a sheep, and kill it, or sell it; he shall restore five oxen for an ox, and four sheep for a sheep. If a thief be found breaking up, and be smitten that he die, there shall no blood be shed for him. If the sun be risen upon him, there shall be blood shed for him; for he should make full restitution; if he have nothing, then he shall be sold for his theft. If the theft be certainly found in his hand alive, whether it be ox, or ass, or sheep; he shall restore double. (Exodus 22:1–4)

Theft of assets before being prosecuted and before a sin offering can be accepted:

Speak unto the children of Israel, When a man or woman shall commit any sin that men commit, to do a trespass against the LORD, and that person be guilty; Then they shall confess their sin which they have done: and he shall recompense his trespass with the principal thereof, and add unto it the fifth part thereof, and give it unto him against whom he hath trespassed. (Numbers 5:6, 7)

Negligent property damage:

If a man shall cause a field or vineyard to be eaten, and shall put in his beast, and shall feed in another man's field; of the best of his own field, and of the best of his own vineyard, shall he make restitution. If fire break out, and catch in thorns, so that the stacks of corn, or the standing corn, or the field, be consumed therewith; he that kindled the fire shall surely make restitution. (Exodus 22:5, 6)

Breach of trust or negligence in stewardship:

If a man shall deliver unto his neighbour money or stuff to keep, and it be stolen out of the man's house; if the thief be found, let him pay double. If the thief be not found, then the master of the house shall be brought unto the judges, to see whether he have put his hand unto his neighbour's goods. For all manner of trespass, whether it be for ox, for ass, for sheep, for raiment, or for any manner of lost thing, which another challengeth to be his, the cause of both parties shall come before the judges; and whom the judges shall condemn, he shall pay double unto his neighbour. If a man deliver unto his neighbour an ass, or an ox, or a sheep, or any beast, to keep; and it die, or be hurt, or driven away, no man seeing it: Then shall an oath of the LORD be between them both, that he hath not put his hand unto his neighbour's goods; and the owner of it shall accept thereof, and he shall not make it good. And if it be stolen from him, he shall make restitution unto the owner thereof. If it be torn in pieces, then let him bring it for witness, and he shall not make good that which was torn. (Exodus 22:7–13)

Damage of something borrowed:

And if a man borrow ought of his neighbour, and it be hurt, or die, the owner thereof being not with it, he shall surely make it good. But if the owner thereof be with it, he shall not make it good: if it be an hired thing, it came for his hire. (Exodus 22:14, 15)

Seduction of a maid:

And if a man entice a maid that is not betrothed, and lie with her, he shall surely endow her to be his wife. If her father utterly refuse to give her unto him, he shall pay money according to the dowry of virgins. (Exodus 22:16, 17)

2. **Crimes meriting the death penalty—hanging**

Most crimes in the Mosaic law that require the death penalty specify how the person is to be put to death, but some do not specify. When the death penalty is required, but the manner of execution is not given, hanging is the prescribed manner:

And if a man have committed a sin worthy of death, and he be to be put to death, and thou hang him on a tree: His body shall not remain all night upon the tree, but thou shalt in any wise bury him that day; (for he that is hanged is accursed of God;) that thy land be not defiled, which the LORD thy God giveth thee for an inheritance. (Deuteronomy 21:22, 23)

Negligence resulting in death:

If an ox gore a man or a woman, that they die: then the ox shall be surely stoned, and his flesh shall not be eaten; but the owner of the ox shall be quit. But if the ox were wont to push with his horn in time past, and it hath been testified to his owner, and he hath not kept him in, but that he hath killed a man or a woman; the ox shall be stoned, and his owner also shall be put to death. If there be laid on him a sum of money, then he shall give for the ransom of his life whatsoever is laid upon him. Whether he have gored a son, or have gored a daughter, according to this judgment shall it be done unto him. (Exodus 21:28–31)

First- and second-degree murder:

He that smiteth a man, so that he die, shall be surely put to death. (Exodus 21:12)

Whoso killeth any person, the murderer shall be put to death by the mouth of witnesses: but one witness shall not testify against any person *to cause him* to die. Moreover ye shall take no satisfaction for the life of a murderer, which *is* guilty of death: but he shall be surely put to death. (Numbers 35:30, 31)

Kidnapping:

And he that stealeth a man, and selleth him, or if he be found in his hand, he shall surely be put to death. (Exodus 21:16)

3. **Crimes meriting the death penalty—stoning**

One key difference between hanging and stoning is that in the latter case, the people are required to participate in administering justice. The crimes that merit stoning go beyond the interaction of two individuals. These third-category offenses are also offenses against the community; therefore, the community is required to participate in the eradication of the evil.

Working on the Sabbath:

> Six days may work be done; but in the seventh is the sabbath of rest, holy to the LORD: whosoever doeth any work in the sabbath day, he shall surely be put to death. (Exodus 31:15)

> Six days shall work be done, but on the seventh day there shall be to you an holy day, a sabbath of rest to the LORD: whosoever doeth work therein shall be put to death. (Exodus 35:2)

[Notice that working on the Sabbath, with its requisite punishment, is one of the few crimes in the law repeated three times. The other is disrespecting parents.]

> And they that found him gathering sticks brought him unto Moses and Aaron, and unto all the congregation. And they put him in ward, because it was not declared what should be done to him. And the LORD said unto Moses, The man shall be surely put to death: all the congregation shall stone him with stones without the camp. And all the congregation brought him without the camp, and stoned him with stones. (Numbers 15:33–36)

Idolatry:

> He that sacrificeth unto any god, save unto the LORD only, he shall be utterly destroyed. (Exodus 22:20)

> But thou shalt surely kill him; thine hand shall be first upon him to put him to death, and afterwards the hand of all the people. And thou shalt stone him with stones, that he die; because he hath sought to thrust thee away from the LORD thy God, which brought thee out of the land of Egypt, from the house of bondage. (Deuteronomy 13:9, 10)

Child sacrifice:

> Again, thou shalt say to the children of Israel, Whosoever he be of the children of Israel, or of the strangers that sojourn in Israel, that giveth any of his seed unto Molech; he shall surely be put to death: the people of the land shall stone him with stones. (Leviticus 20:2)

[This provision gives us a clearer insight into how the Lord views abortion. This crime is not unlike the offering of children on the altar of lust—the altar of Molech.]

Necromancy, witchcraft, and wizardry:

> A man also or woman that hath a familiar spirit, or that is a wizard, shall surely be put to death: they shall stone them with stones: their blood shall be upon them. (Leviticus 20:27)

Thou shalt not suffer a witch to live. (Exodus 22:18)

Blasphemy:

> And he that blasphemeth the name of the LORD, he shall surely be put to death, and all the congregation shall certainly stone him: as well the stranger, as he that is born in the land, when he blasphemeth the name of the LORD, shall be put to death. (Leviticus 24:16)

Disrespecting a parent:

> And he that smiteth his father, or his mother, shall be surely put to death.... And he that curseth his father, or his mother, shall surely be put to death. (Exodus 22:15, 17)

> For every one that curseth his father or his mother shall be surely put to death: he hath cursed his father or his mother; his blood shall be upon him. (Leviticus 20:9)

> If a man have a stubborn and rebellious son, which will not obey the voice of his father, or the voice of his mother, and that, when they have chastened him, will not hearken unto them: Then shall his father and his mother lay hold on him, and bring him out unto the elders of his city, and unto the gate of his place; And they shall say unto the elders of his city, This our son is stubborn and rebellious, he will not obey our voice; he is a glutton, and a drunkard. And all the men of his city shall stone him with stones, that he die: so shalt thou put evil away from among you; and all Israel shall hear, and fear. (Deuteronomy 21:18–21)

Sexual sins:

   A. *Adultery:*

Then ye shall bring them both out unto the gate of that city, and ye shall stone them with stones that they die; the damsel, because she cried not, being in the city; and the man, because he hath humbled his neighbour's wife: so thou shalt put away evil from among you. (Deuteronomy 22:24)

   B. *Incest:*

And the man that lieth with his father's wife hath uncovered his father's nakedness: both of them shall surely be put to death; their blood shall be upon them. And if a man lie with his daughter in law, both of them shall surely be put to death: they have wrought confusion; their blood shall be upon them. (Leviticus 20:11, 12)

   C. *Bestiality:*

And if a man lie with a beast, he shall surely be put to death: and ye shall slay the beast. And if a woman approach unto any beast, and lie down thereto, thou shalt kill the woman, and the beast: they shall surely be put to death; their blood shall be upon them. (Leviticus 20:15, 16)

Whosoever lieth with a beast shall surely be put to death. (Exodus 22:19)

   D. *Sodomy:*

If a man also lie with mankind, as he lieth with a woman, both of them have committed an abomination: they shall surely be put to death; their blood shall be upon them. (Leviticus 20:13)

   E. *Prostitution:*

Then they shall bring out the damsel to the door of her father's house, and the men of her city shall stone her with stones that she die: because she hath wrought folly in Israel, to play the whore in her father's house: so shalt thou put evil away from among you. (Deuteronomy 22:21)

4. **Crimes meriting the death penalty—by fire**

Polygamy with both the wife and her mother:

And if a man take a wife and her mother, it is wickedness: they shall be burnt with fire, both he and they; that there be no wickedness among you. (Leviticus 20:14)

Prostitution of the priest's daughter:

> And the daughter of any priest, if she profane herself by playing the whore, she profaneth her father: she shall be burnt with fire. (Leviticus 21:9)

The Severest Punishment Is a Glorious Deliverance

The severest punishment in Scripture is described in the third angel's message, where God graciously warns humanity that whoever worships the beast and his image or receives his mark will suffer His wrath, unmixed with mercy (see Rev. 14:9–11). Why such severity? Because of the severity of the offense: blasphemy coupled with idolatry in willful submission to and worship of the most evil tyranny that ever existed.

Babylon and the beast she rides will be a despotic, demonic power controlled by avarice, pride, and the basest lusts, and if allowed by God, this duo would readily commit the worst genocide of the righteous in human history. Astride the beast, Babylon the Great is depicted as "the habitation of devils, and the hold of every foul spirit, and a cage of every unclean and hateful bird" (Rev. 18:2).

Someone might be asking, What does this most severe punishment look like? God is explicit. All offenders "shall be tormented with fire and brimstone in the presence of the holy angels and in the presence of the Lamb" (14:10, 11). It is no coincidence that this severest of punishments combines 1) brimstone *and* 2) fire and does this 3) in the presence of heaven, not unlike the most serious offenses in Israel, which required 1) stoning and 2) fire that were inflicted 3) in the presence of and by the congregation. However, notice the divine severity: This is not just a pelting of stones, but a horrific hail of burning, sulfuric boulders combined with unquenchable, devouring fire, not just in the presence of mortals, but in the presence of holy angels who excel in strength and the devouring presence of the Lamb.

> And as the oppression of the remnant by Babylon and the beast will be more severe than was the oppression of the Hebrews (like Israel did, the pure woman will flee into the wilderness and, for a time, be pursued and hunted there by the harlot). the deliverance will be all the more remarkable and joyful:

The Lion and Lamb are combined in Revelation, but, significantly, in meting out the punishment of Babylon and the beast, the merciful Lamb is the One who sees to it that justice is fully served. This is the same Lamb that was in the cloud when the sea closed over the armies of Egypt. This event was a foreshadowing of the final, more glorious deliverance of God's people at the end. And as the oppression of the remnant by Babylon and the beast will be more severe than was the oppression of the Hebrews (like Israel did, the pure woman will flee into the wilderness and, for a time, be pursued and hunted there by the harlot). the deliverance will be all the more remarkable and joyful:

> And after these things I heard a great voice of much people in heaven, saying, Alleluia; Salvation, and glory, and honour, and power, unto the Lord our God: For true and righteous are his judgments: for he hath judged the great whore, which did corrupt the earth with her fornication, and hath avenged the blood of his servants at her hand. And again they said, Alleluia. And her smoke rose up for ever and ever. And the four and twenty elders and the four beasts fell down and worshipped God that sat on the throne, saying, Amen; Alleluia. And a voice came out of the throne, saying, Praise our God, all ye his servants, and ye that fear him, both small and great.
>
> And I heard as it were the voice of a great multitude, and as the voice of many waters, and as the voice of mighty thunderings, saying, Alleluia: for the Lord God omnipotent reigneth. Let us be glad and rejoice, and give honour to him: for the marriage of the Lamb is come, and his wife hath made herself ready. And to her was granted that she should be arrayed in fine linen, clean and white: for the fine linen is the righteousness of saints.
>
> And he saith unto me, Write, Blessed are they which are called unto the marriage supper of the Lamb. And he saith unto me, These are the true sayings of God.... I Jesus have sent mine angel to testify unto you these things in the churches. I am the root and the offspring of David, *and* the bright and morning star. And the Spirit and the bride say, Come. And let him that heareth say, Come. And let him that is athirst come. And whosoever will, let him take the water of life freely.... He which testifieth these things saith, Surely I come quickly. Amen. Even so, come, Lord Jesus. The grace of our Lord Jesus Christ *be* with you all. Amen. (Revelation 19:1–9; 22:16, 17, 20, 21)

***

For more studies on Daniel and Revelation, the sealing of the covenant, and the final atonement of Christ, see the author's companion book, *The Final Atonement*, also published by TEACH Services.

Bibliography

"French Republican calendar." Wikipedia. https://1ref.us/mset3. Accessed May 4, 2023.

"List of natural disasters in the United States." Wikipedia. https://1ref.us/mset4. Accessed May 4, 2023.

"Scala Sancta." Wikipedia. https://1ref.us/mset5. Accessed May 4, 2023.

White, Ellen G. *The Great Controversy*. Mountain View, CA: Pacific Press Publishing Association, 1911.

———. *Life Sketches of Ellen G. White*. Mountain View, CA: Pacific Press Publishing Association, 1915.

———. *Manuscript Releases*. Vol. 1. Silver Spring, MD: Ellen G. White Estate, 1981.

———. *Manuscript Releases*. Vol. 2. Silver Spring, MD: Ellen G. White Estate, 1987.

———. *Manuscript Releases*. Vol. 12. Silver Spring, MD: Ellen G. White Estate, 1990.

———. *Manuscript Releases*. Vol. 19. Silver Spring, MD: Ellen G. White Estate, 1990.

———. *Manuscript Releases*. Vol. 21. Silver Spring, MD: Ellen G. White Estate, 1993.

———. *Temperance*. Mountain View, CA: Pacific Press Publishing Association, 1949.

———. *Testimonies for the Church*. Vol. 8. Mountain View, CA: Pacific Press Publishing Association, 1904.

———. *Testimonies to Ministers and Gospel Workers*. Mountain View, CA: Pacific Press Publishing Association, 1923.

TEACH Services, Inc.
P U B L I S H I N G

We invite you to view the complete
selection of titles we publish at:
www.TEACHServices.com

We encourage you to write us
with your thoughts about this,
or any other book we publish at:
info@TEACHServices.com

TEACH Services' titles may be purchased in
bulk quantities for educational, fund-raising,
business, or promotional use.
bulksales@TEACHServices.com

Finally, if you are interested in seeing
your own book in print, please contact us at:
publishing@TEACHServices.com
We are happy to review your manuscript at no charge.

www.ingramcontent.com/pod-product-compliance
Lightning Source LLC
Chambersburg PA
CBHW050802160426
43192CB00010B/1615